D1511192

CULTURES OF AMERICA

AFRICAN AMERICANS

By Shelia Payton

Marshall Cavendish
New York • London • Toronto

Published by
Marshall Cavendish Corporation
2415 Jerusalem Avenue
P.0. Box 587
North Bellmore, New York 11710, U.S.A.

© Marshall Cavendish Corporation, 1995

Edited, designed, and produced by Water Buffalo Books, Milwaukee

All rights reserved. No part of this book may be reproduced or utilized in any form or by any means electronic or mechanical, including photocopying or recording, or by any information storage and retrieval system, without permission from the copyright holders.

Project director: Mark Sachner
Art director: Sabine Beaupré
Picture researcher: Diane Laska
Editorial: Valerie Weber
Marshall Cavendish development editor: MaryLee Knowlton
Marshall Cavendish editorial director: Evelyn Fazio

Water Buffalo Books would like to acknowledge The Eternal Light Community Singers and their director, Selwyn Rawls, Harlem, New York, shown on page 4.

Picture Credits: Sabine Beaupré 1994: 7, 19; © The Bettmann Archive: 18, 23, 24, 27, 39, 62 (left), 64 (top), 65 (bottom right); © Cheryl L. Franklin, Milwaukee, Wisconsin: 28, 29, 35, 40, 45, 46, 48, 52, 53 (both), 57 (bottom); © Arlene Gottfried: 4, 36, 37, 38, 54 (left); © Hazel Hankin: 1, 34, 57 (top), 58, 59; © Shelia Payton: 6, 9, 10, 56; © Reuters/ Bettmann Archive: 32 (right), 33 (top), 42, 43, 67, 72, 74 (top); © Springer/Bettmann Film Archive: 64 (bottom), 66, 68; © 1994 The Stock Market/John Pinderhughes: Cover; © UPI/Bettmann: 8, 11, 32 (left), 33 (bottom), 41, 47, 50 (both), 54 (right), 60, 62 (right), 65 (top and bottom left), 69, 70, 71, 73, 74 (bottom)

Library of Congress Cataloging-in-Publication Data

Payton, Shelia.
    African Americans / Shelia Payton.
       p.   cm. — (Cultures of America)
    Includes bibliographical references and index.
    ISBN 1-85435-780-8 (set). — ISBN 1-85435-787-5 : $19.95
    1. Afro-Americans—Juvenile literature. I. Title. II. Series.
    E185.P38 1995
    305.896'073—dc20   94-12631
                                     CIP
                                     AC

To PS – MS

Printed and bound in the U.S.A.

CONTENTS

INTRODUCTION

The story of African Americans is the story of achievement against the odds. Perhaps more than any other ethnic group in this country, African Americans have had to overcome tremendous obstacles not only to succeed, but also to survive. The majority were brought to this country under some of the most brutal and inhumane conditions in history. Denied their humanity, treated as property, facing daily efforts to strip them of their culture and heritage, laboring without pay for over three hundred years, facing open discrimination for nearly four hundred years, and facing both open and more subtle discrimination even to this day, African Americans have nonetheless continued to help build a nation, an economy, and a culture that is second to none in the world.

They have helped establish and preserve democracy by fighting in wars for freedom, even when they themselves were not free. They have given this country and the world art forms that are unique and respected across racial and ethnic lines. They have used their intellect to help save lives and improve the quality of life through inventions and scientific and medical discoveries. They have brought a vibrancy — a style — to life in this country that has helped tint the world of the Puritans into a rainbow of color and growing appreciation for ethnic diversity. They have opened the doors for other ethnic groups and women by fighting for their freedom from slavery and discrimination.

Too often, African Americans have not received credit for what they have done and are doing. Too often, only the negative images of African American life are projected to the larger world. But despite attempts to deny their contributions, African Americans in this country continue to survive, contribute, and leave their imprint on American and world culture alike.

What accounts for this determined spirit? Perhaps it is a reflection of the deep spiritual ground upon which African American culture rests, even today. Perhaps it is a reflection of the human spirit in all of us that refuses to give up. Whatever the reason, there can be no question about this: African Americans are the descendants not just of slaves, they are the descendants of the survivors.

A Senegalese girl walks along the coast of West Africa, the ancestral homeland of many African Americans.

CHAPTER ONE

LEAVING A HOMELAND
AFRICAN SEED

As Kunta Kinte walked among the mangrove trees looking for just the right tree trunk to cut and make into a drum, he had no way of knowing he would never see his mother or his village of Juffure in Gambia, West Africa, again. A crack of a branch was the only warning he had before a group of men — white and Black — attacked him and carried him away to live the rest of his life as a slave.

The story of Kunta Kinte and his descendants is the story of more than twenty-five million Americans of African origin. It was told by the late Alex Haley in his book *Roots*. That book became a bestseller, and a television miniseries based on the book attracted the largest audience in TV history.

What gave Kunta Kinte's story such power is the fact that Haley was able to trace his family back to the original village. Unfortunately, most African Americans will never know the identity of the first ancestor to arrive in this country, and they will never be able to find their cousins in Africa. Most African Americans can only hope to narrow their search down to an ethnic group or country of origin. Even finding the exact country or ethnic group from which their ancestors came is difficult, because during the slave trade, people from the same ethnic group or community were often intentionally separated and put together with people from

other African ethnic groups to lessen the possibility of revolt. As a result, slaves often married and had children with slaves from another ethnic group, or they might intermarry with American Indians. Also, children were born as a result of relationships (many of them forced) with Europeans, either during the trip over or on the plantation. This would make determining origins based on individual appearances more difficult.

The Common Fabric: Africa's West Coast

What is known, based on information about the slave trade, is that most slaves came

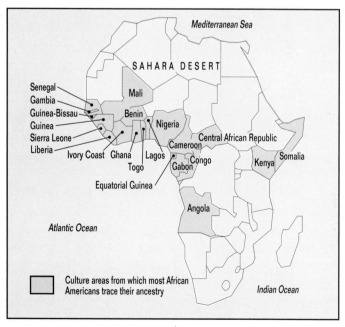

Most Africans brought to America as slaves were from West Africa. Many also came from Central Africa.

7

African Americans can trace their ancestry to a number of West African countries, including Ghana.

from Africa's West Coast — from countries later known as Benin, Cameroon, Dahomey, Gabon, Gambia, Ghana, Guinea, the Ivory Coast, Nigeria, Senegal, Sierra Leone, Togo, and parts of the Congo. Because they are so close to the equator, these countries are part of what has also been called equatorial Africa. The countries are located along the route used since the 1400s by European sailors who were trying to reach India, Cathay (now known as China), and Mali — countries that were rumored to have great wealth.

The route to these countries, which carried European ships south around the Cape of Good Hope at the tip of Africa and then north into the Indian Ocean, was the long way around. But land routes were controlled first by Arabs and then by Turks, who made safe, easy passage to Africa and India along Mediterranean roads difficult.

While similarities in language, religion, agriculture, and political organization in these African countries suggest a common origin, there are some differences. The coastal cultures can be roughly divided into three regions: the Western Su-

GOLD PUTS MALI ON THE MAP

In 1324, Mansa Musa, the emperor of Mali, traveled to Mecca, the holy city for Muslims. The trip became the talk of Africa, Europe, and Arabia. Emperor Musa is reported to have taken anywhere from eight thousand to fifteen thousand people with him on the trip. According to accounts, this included five hundred slaves carrying gold staffs that weighed six pounds each. The slaves marched at the head of this mass of humanity. Behind them rode the emperor on horseback, and behind him followed camels carrying yet more gold. In Cairo, Emperor Musa is said to have spent so much gold that it caused the price of the precious metal to drop 12 percent. It took several years for the Cairo gold market to recover after the emperor of Mali left. Shortly after that display of wealth, Mali began to appear on European maps.

dan (which includes Senegal and significant parts of Ghana, Ivory Coast, Sierra Leone, and Guinea), the West African Rain Forest (which includes parts of Senegal, Dahomey, Togo, Ghana, Guinea, Nigeria, and Benin), and the Bantu States (which include Cameroon, Gabon, and Congo).

Much of Black African civilization grew out of the culture created by people who moved from the southern Sahara Desert to the Sudan — a grassy plain (called a savanna) that stretches one thousand miles south of the Sahara between the Atlantic Ocean, the Indian Ocean, and the Red Sea. From the Sudan, these people moved to almost every other part of Africa.

The Sudan civilization existed more than one thousand years before the creation of the ancient empire of Ghana, which began in about A.D. 300. Much of this civilization is believed to have grown out of the culture of the Mande-speaking people (also know as the

Mandika or Mandingo people). The Mande shaped ideas about agriculture, social structure, political organization, warfare, and religion.

Village Life. Typically, the Mande lived in villages of five hundred to three thousand people. A few villages had populations of ten to twenty thousand; and some villages, located in key trade areas, served as state capitals. These towns had populations of thirty to forty thousand people. The homes in these villages were clustered together in compounds made up of a family head and his married sons. Villages were surrounded by fields that the people used to grow their crops.

The typical home was not fancy, but it was comfortable. It usually contained a cot, rugs, stools, and wooden or woven chests for storing such tools as bows and arrows, spears, axes, hoes, baskets, pots, stones for grinding millet and sorghum into meal, and scythes for cutting down grain, as well as nicer clothes

These homes in Senegal shelter their occupants from the midday sun.

For centuries, wrestling and other sports have helped teach West African military skills.

to support the king and his court, traders, artisans, and small standing armies. These farming methods also allowed them to grow crops without having to work in the fields every day.

In addition to tending the crops, men also took care of cattle, sheep, and goats. In their free time, they built and repaired homes, made tools, served in the military or worked on special projects for the nation, and took part in local government affairs.

Mande women also worked hard. They harvested the crops and grew vegetables on small plots of land near their village. In addition, they kept house, cooked, took care of the children, made pots and baskets, looked after the poultry, and traded their crops for food and other items they needed.

Each village had a market where people traded for what they needed. Until the 1900s, most buying and selling was done by trading things rather than with money. In larger cities, however, cowrie shells, bars of copper or iron, gold, cotton, and even some written draft notes were used as money.

While the economy in the fertile areas of the Mande/Sudan civilization was based on agriculture, in the major portion of the region, trade was the basis of wealth. That trade involved gold, iron, ivory, cloth, hides, spices, and slaves. Much of the wealth that came from this trade was used to support the nation and the king and his court.

Religion. Mande/Sudan society was complex in its religious, social, and political struc-

and other personal items. The Mande and many other people living in the Sudan region wore elaborately woven cloth breeches, tunics, and sandals at a time when other people living in the coastal areas were either naked or wore breeches made of bark.

The Mande diet consisted mainly of millet, rice, or sorghum seasoned with peppers and spices. Some Mande drank cow or goat milk or made cheese from the milk. Leafy vegetables and wild fruit rounded out the diet. Famine was almost unknown.

The Mande were skilled farmers, and the civilization they helped create was almost exclusively agricultural for at least two thousand years. Mande men did most of the farm work in the field surrounding the village. They pulled the wild grass and weeds out of the ground, tilled the soil, and built dikes and earthen dams to help water the crops. The Mande also rotated their crops — letting fields lie vacant — to keep from destroying the soil.

These farming techniques allowed the Mande to raise enough food not only to feed themselves and their families, but also

ture. The religious life of the community centered on the belief that good behavior, prayer, and regularly following rituals and making offerings were important to ensuring a good life. While they believed God created the universe and the laws that control nature and human behavior, they also believed God did not get involved in people's day-to-day lives. For that reason, the Mande addressed prayers and offerings to dead relatives. Praying to ancestors was considered a key ingredient in religion and morality. Because they were part of the spirit world, dead relatives were believed to be closer to God than those who were living. And because these dead relatives were still part of the family, the Mande believed they would understand the problems their living relatives were experiencing — and do a good job of presenting these problems to God. Dead relatives would

not help the living just because they were part of the family, however. That help had to be earned. To receive it, a man had to live up to his family obligations. If he did not, the ancestors might punish him by making his crops or business fail or allowing problems to develop in family relationships. For this reason, prayers and offerings were made to these spirits on special occasions, such as during planting time.

The Mande also believed that God lived in or visited certain rivers, trees, mountains, and rocks and sometimes appeared in human form — particularly in dreams.

This traditional religion and belief system remained in place for centuries. With trade came contact with other cultures and religions, however, such as Islam, which was practiced by Arab merchants from North Africa. Slaves who worked for these mer-

Women in Nigeria and other West African countries are both homemakers and workers outside of the home. In rural areas, they help harvest and sell crops.

chants were probably the first to be converted to Islam. Some Black African merchants might also have converted for either religious or business reasons. Islam did not really begin to grow, however, until the first African kings accepted the religion in the eleventh century. At that time, the religion began to spread among members of the royal court. Even so, most ordinary citizens continued to practice the traditional African religion.

War: Only When Necessary. Sometimes states went to war either to defend themselves against others or to capture the additional land or goods they needed to maintain their strengthen and power. Wars were not fought for the glory of defeating or wiping out another ethnic group. Nor did the culture support the idea that it was better to die in a hopeless cause than to run from a fight. In fact, it was accepted, if not expected, that soldiers would retreat in battles when the tide turned against them.

The kingdoms rarely had standing armies. Instead, men from the villages came together to fight when war was declared and went home to take care of their regular duties when the war was over.

The people who were defeated in war paid taxes to the victors, maintained their roads, provided troops for the emperor's army, provided laborers to work on special projects, and sometimes paid the state gold, copper, or gems. In exchange, they received protection from aggressive neighbors, help in maintaining law and order, and guarantees of trade rights and safe passage for goods. Generally speaking, the people in the conquered states were not required to adopt the language or culture of the winners.

The influence of Mande/Sudan civilization produced empires throughout western Africa. Not surprisingly, the first to appear were in the Western Sudan region.

Western Sudan

For centuries of its history, the Western Sudan was part of powerful African empires that rivaled or surpassed Europe in wealth, power, and culture. The wealth and power of these kingdoms resulted from their strategic location between the Mediterranean Sea and the gold deposits in West Africa.

Arabs had to cross the Sahara Desert and travel through these kingdoms to get to the West African gold deposits. The Arab merchants paid a custom fee for the goods entering and leaving the kingdom in exchange for a military escort to protect them from thieves.

A DIFFERENT KIND OF SLAVERY

Slavery in Africa was not the same as slavery in America. Slaves were treated more like servants or members of the family. The people who were enslaved were usually those captured in war.

Unlike slaves in this country, they were not a despised group, and they even had rights — especially if they achieved a high position in the king's service. Children born to slaves who were in the king's service, for example, could not be sold. They might perform business or diplomatic tasks for the king.

In some instances, well-trained slave troops or commanders led armies into wars on behalf of the king. And some kings appointed slaves to serve as governors and tax collectors in conquered areas.

Strict controls in the markets ensured that no one was cheated and people paid their debts.

Traders traveling between the Mediterranean and the West African mines brought salt with them from North Africa, which was almost impossible to find in West Africa. The little salt that was available was made from evaporating sea water. This process was expensive, and the salt had to be carried long distances back to the villages, where people used it to both flavor and preserve their food. On the other hand, salt was plentiful in the Sahara.

Slabs of salt were mined and taken by camel to the markets in the Sudan, where they were sold in exchange for gold. Gold was plentiful south of the Sudan — especially in what is now Ghana and Guinea. In addition to gold and salt, other goods such as pepper, kola nuts, elephant tusks, millet, sorghum, iron bars, and leather were brought into markets throughout the kingdom of Ghana and traded for cloth, metalwork, silk, and other goods from North Africa.

In addition to farming and trade, the Sudan civilization was involved in mining, smelting, and forging iron centuries before the birth of Christ. The iron was used to make arrows, hoe blades, and axe heads, which were used to cut down trees so the Sudan farmers could clear land to plant crops. This ability to clear the land helped encourage migration to the forest region, which resulted in another variation on the Sudan civilization — the West African Rain Forest culture.

West African Rain Forest

The West African Rain Forest is a long, narrow belt south of Sudan that stretches almost uninterrupted from modern Senegal to the Congo Basin. The only break in the forest is in Togo and Benin, where grasslands run down to the Atlantic Ocean.

The forest was made up of giant hardwood trees that grew so close together the sun never reached the ground. Part of this area (in the lowland coastal regions of Guinea, Liberia, and Nigeria) contained swamps and jungles. But most of the forest grew in hilly upland regions a few miles from the coast, near rivers that fed into the ocean.

Village Life. Because clearing the forest was difficult, those who settled in the Rain Forest lived in compact villages of five hundred to ten thousand people. Many of those who settled in the Rain Forest were Akan-speaking people, who are believed to be descendants of Egyptians or the Kush people, who lived at least two thousand years before Christ in a region just south of the current Sudan-Egypt border. The Akan now live primarily in southern Ghana and the Ivory Coast.

During the early settlement of the Rain Forest, the villages and towns were made up of quarters where people from different clans or ethnic groups lived together. These compounds of extended families were formed around a marketplace or common area. Each day, the men walked from the towns to their gardens located in small clearings under the trees, where they grew root, or underground, plants. They used hoes to weed and plant their crops. In larger Rain Forest towns, these fields were several miles away. Rather than walk to the field every day, the men would often build small shelters near the fields and stay there for several days.

Because there were no donkeys, camels, horses, elephants, or other beasts of burden in the Rain Forest, men and women had to carry loads of produce from the fields to their towns during harvest time. Part of this food was kept for the family, and the rest was sold or exchanged for other needed items.

A Creative People. In addition to farming, the Rain Forest people were masters at mining and smelting metals, including iron.

They also were masters of creativity. Art and music flourished in the Rain Forest. In fact, the art of the Forest people is considered the best in Black Africa. Powerful and skillfully made wood carvings were common. Another art form was sculpture made primarily out of bronze, stone, and clay. Among ethnic groups such as the Ife and Benin, bronze and clay sculptures portray complex religious themes. The tradition of sculpting is thousands of years old. In their work, the artists' focus is on expressing their feelings rather than trying to produce an exact copy of an object. This expressionist approach later provided the basis for works by American and European artists. European artists such as Picasso and Modigliani borrowed images and ideas from African art.

The music of this region has also had a broad impact. It is the foundation for jazz and popular music in the United States and the Caribbean.

Theater was another art form that flourished among the Rain Forest people. Professional actors and musicians traveled from town to town, putting on plays based on popular moral and religious themes.

The Rain Forest civilization was based on speech rather than the written word. People did not write down their stories or history; rather, they passed them from one generation to the next by telling and retelling stories. Using this method, the culture produced thousands of proverbs, parables, morality tales, and funny stories, which were recited to audiences by accomplished storytellers. Many of these stories (like the tales of Brer Rabbit)

were brought to the United States by slaves and became part of the African American folklore tradition. Oral historians kept the history of the people alive by spending hours retelling the adventures and achievements of great kings.

Religion and Politics. Religion also flourished in the Rain Forest. Priests and scholars helped keep the intellectual life of the community fresh and alive by debating religious and philosophical questions.

The religion practiced by the Rain Forest people was similar to that of the Mande/Sudan civilization, with almost no influence from Islam. The people believed their ancestors were responsible for controlling nature. They built shrines in their villages and compounds that were usually decorated with wood or stone sculptures symbolizing the spirits of their ancestors.

Much of the political life of the Rain Forest people was also similar to that of the Mande/Sudan civilization. The idea of a king as ruler existed in the 1400s, before the Europeans arrived. As was the case in Mande/Sudan civilization, these kings were believed to be divine or to have access to the divine.

The Asante: A Military Way of Life. One of the most powerful states in the Rain Forest belonged to the Asante. The Asante state (located mainly in Ghana) differed from the Mande/Sudan state in several ways.

First of all, it established a national army whose military philosophy was to keep fighting until they pushed the enemy back. Because the forest was so dense, the military was primarily made up of infantry (foot soldiers) instead of cavalry (horsemen). The empire did add cavalry to its army, however, after it conquered some of its neighbors in the Sudan.

The reputation of the Asante for being fierce warriors was so strong that when King

Opoku Ware captured the trading centers of Elmina (built by the Portuguese in the 1400s) and Apollonia (built by the Dutch in the 1600s), those countries agreed to rent the land from the empire rather than fight a war. The Asante also took over the city of Accra, which is now the capital of Ghana. This gave them access to the guns, gunpowder, and manufactured goods they needed to maintain control over their empire.

A major reason for the success of the Asante empire was its ability to quickly adapt its military style to include new ideas, people, and techniques without weakening its system. During the 1800s, the Asante employed scribes, military trainers, skilled craftsmen, and commercial advisors from Hausaland (the rain forest of southern Nigeria) and Volta (the area at the headwater of the Volta River in the Western Sudan) and from Europe to help them run their empire.

The military way of life became essential to maintaining the Asante empire. Playing sports and practicing the use of weapons were nearly a national pastime.

The second significant difference between the Sudan civilization and the Asante is that the Asante insisted all the conquered people adopt their culture.

The Asante continued to dominate until their neighbors, the Fante, teamed up with the British to defeat them in the 1800s. The Asante had been warring with the Fante since 1806, fearing the Fante might cut off their access to the sea. By 1874, the Fante/British military had reduced the Asante empire to the size it was before King Opoku Ware began his expansion campaign.

The Yoruba. Like the Asante, the Yoruba were a significant ethnic group living in the Rain Forest region. In fact, they were among the most organized people on the African continent. The Yoruba, believed to have originated in the city of Ife (in southern Nigeria), lived in villages and cities, many of them with populations of one hundred thousand people. There is evidence that as far back as 400 B.C., the Yoruba had mastered the skills of smelting iron, ironwork, and agriculture.

While the Yoruba people share the same language and dress, similar social and political systems, and acknowledge common origins, the culture of groups who live on the grasslands of the Sudan differs somewhat from the culture of the people who live in the forest. The grasslands Yoruba culture is very similar to that of the rest of the Sudan. Their economy was based on agriculture, as it is today, and they grew the same crops as others in the Sudan region. The grassland Yoruba focused their attention on politics and government more so than on the development of the arts.

The forest Yoruba culture, on the other hand, tended to follow the pattern of the Rain Forest. These Yoruba lived in large villages and cities, developed a rich arts culture, and grew those underground crops that survived best in the humid environment of the forest.

The Edo, Benin, and Dahomey. East of the Yoruba on the Guinea coast lived the Edo people of Benin, who developed one of the most powerful and highly developed states in the Guinea forest. Benin bronze sculpture, which may be found in museums in Europe, is regarded as among the most magnificent in the world.

Because it was located not too far from the ocean on a river that boats could easily navigate, Benin began trading with Europe around 1485. In the 1500s, the Portuguese sent traders and missionaries to Benin. And in 1553, the first Englishman to visit Benin discovered that the king spoke Portuguese. Trade with Europe did not last long, however, because the weather and health conditions of the region did not agree with the European traders who had established trading stations there. These traders decided to concentrate their efforts on Dahomey.

Dahomey's power grew out of the slave trade. In fact, Europeans called Dahomey the Slave Coast because it controlled most of the coast and the European slave trade. Many of these slaves were people from the Fon group — an Ewe-speaking population that lived in loosely organized societies in Dahomey.

Dahomey was organized along military lines. The king had absolute power and was also the high priest of the country. He appointed all military officers and all administrators in the country and required absolute loyalty from them. Because the country was poor and had a small population (fewer than two hundred thousand people), Dahomey engaged in wars of conquest to protect itself against its enemies.

Being in a state of constant war led to two conditions that differed considerably from the Sudan civilization: large numbers of human sacrifices and a significant number of women serving in the government and the military.

While human sacrifice did happen occasionally in the Sudan civilization, it was rare. In Dahomey, however, criminals and captured slaves were sacrificed in large numbers to ensure the help of the ancestors in the country's quest for wealth. The belief was that human life was so valuable that the sacrifice of a human being was the most precious gift the ancestors could be offered.

The use of women in the government grew out of the need to replace men in times of war. Women were usually paired with men to learn how to carry out various government duties. Most of the women were wives or daughters of the king, which helped ensure their loyalty.

Women were also used in the military, where they fought alongside male soldiers. The women's army corps, called the Amazons by Europeans, were considered equal to the men in combat. They had their own female commanders and underwent rigorous training, just as the men did.

The strong military nature of Dahomey made it able to defeat opponents five to ten times its size. But the wealth and power of the country declined when Europe abolished its slave trade.

The Bantu States

The final coastal culture to which the majority of African Americans can trace their roots is found in the Bantu states. Bantu-speakers make up most of the Black African population south of the equator, as well as people living in Somalia, Kenya, Cameroon, the Central African Republic, and Nigeria. They are divided into roughly three hundred different clans.

The first Bantu are believed to have moved from the grasslands near the Nigeria-Cameroon border around the time of Christ. For the most part, the Bantu followed the same farming patterns found in the Sudan region — planting large areas of land one year and letting them lie idle the next year while planting on another large plot of land. They also used many of the same mining, smelting, and forging methods found in other areas of West Africa.

Politically, the Bantu followed a structure that was similar to that of the Sudan civilization — one that depended on the creation of numerous states and small empires.

A LETTER FROM AN AFRICAN KING TO A PORTUGUESE KING

The [Portuguese] merchants are taking every day our natives, sons of the land and sons of our noblemen and vassals and our relatives. . . they grab them and get them to be sold. . . . Your highness should not agree with this nor accept it as in your service.

— from a letter by Congolese King Affonso to King John of Portugal

Like the West African Rain Forest people, the Bantu believed God created the world but did not become involved in humans' everyday lives. For that reason, they believed their ancestors and nature spirits controlled individual fortunes and natural phenomena. The Bantu engaged in complex rituals and made offerings and sacrifices to these spirits to ensure good fortune.

The Congo. One of the most prominent states in the Bantu region was the Congo, which covered a plateau south of the Congo River to northern Angola. At its peak, the Congo extended from the Atlantic to what are now the cities of Kinshasa and Brazzaville. The smallest unit in the Congo political system was the village. Each village was headed by the senior male relative. Villages were organized into districts ruled by chiefs appointed by the king.

Unfortunately, the Bantu did not have a clear line of succession when the king died. As a result, real or ceremonial battles took place to determine who the next king should be. The only requirement was that the would-be king be a descendant of King Wene, the founder of the Congo nation.

This lack of clear succession played a role in the decline of the Congo state. The Portuguese, who first came to the Congo in 1482, introduced Christianity to the family of King Kuwu. When the king's son, Af-fonso, won the battle for the throne, he decided to convert his country to Christianity, thinking it would benefit his people. While the monarch of Portugal and other Portuguese in the Congo supported the idea of a Christian nation under Congolese rule, the Portuguese merchants and sea captains did not.

They intercepted letters from King Affonso to King John of Portugal that complained about the way the merchants were corrupting the Congolese people and kidnapping them to be sold into slavery. The merchants and sea captains intercepted these letters because they did not want King John to interfere with the money they were making by taking slaves to Brazil.

The social disorder caused by these unscrupulous merchants and sea captains, combined with the lack of central control in the Congo, left the country vulnerable to attack. Over the course of several years, unfriendly neighboring states, as well as the Portuguese army based in neighboring Angola, did attack. By the end of the 1800s, the Congo empire no longer existed.

Despite both the slave trade and the decline of many states under European colonial powers, the rich culture of West African civilization lives on — not only in Africa, but also in North America. That civilization is a thread in the fabric we call African American culture.

Although the slave trade was outlawed in 1807, slavery itself existed until the 1860s, leaving a legacy of poverty and racial injustice.

CHAPTER TWO

LIFE IN A NEW LAND
AMERICAN SOIL

The first Africans arrived in America before the *Mayflower,* most likely brought to what is now South Carolina in 1526 by a Spanish explorer. But they ran away to the interior of the state, where they lived with American Indians. In August 1619, twenty Africans, stolen by pirates from a Spanish ship bound for the West Indies, set foot in Jamestown, Virginia, in August 1619 and were exchanged for food by the crew of a Dutch warship. These twenty Africans were treated as indentured servants (people obligated to work for a master for a specified period of time), just as their European counterparts were. Once their term of service was over, they were freed and enjoyed the same rights and privileges as their European working-class counterparts.

The practice of indenture lasted for the first twenty-five years that Africans were in this country. But by 1640, slavery had started to gain a foothold in this country, and it became common to hold Africans past their time of indenture and to make indefinite service the punishment for violating a law — even for a "minor" offense like running away from the master. By the 1650s, chattel slavery — slavery for life — was common. In 1662, slavery became official when Virginia

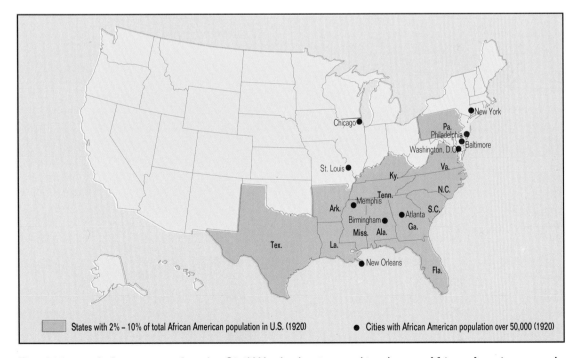

States with 2% – 10% of total African American population in U.S. (1920) • Cities with African American population over 50,000 (1920)

By 1920, nearly forty years after the Civil War had put an end to slavery, African Americans made up a substantial portion of the population of most southern states and several cities in the North.

passed a law using the word *slave* to describe a class of people.

To make matters worse for Africans, Europeans began inventing reasons to justify making Africans slaves. One reason was a false belief that Africans were better suited to work in hot climates because they had built up a resistance to malaria in their homeland.

Skin color also made Africans an easy target for permanent servitude. For one thing, it was impossible for them to run away and disappear into the general population, which was overwhelmingly white. Africans also became objects of prejudice because they looked different and had different cultures. Because they were not Christians, European Americans considered them primitive savages who were only good for doing hard labor. From there, European Americans developed the false belief that Africans were uniquely suited to be slaves. This idea eventually led to the belief that God had put Africans on earth to be slaves to whites.

As the need for labor in the colonies grew, the pressure for slaves grew. Indentured servants had to be freed after their term of service was completed. Slaves did not. An indentured servant, once free, could set up a business or farm that would compete with the former master. Slaves could not. Slaves could be worked to death under conditions a free man would not tolerate. A slaveowner needed only six to seven years of work out of a slave to come out ahead. So slavery became a more appealing labor system.

The Middle Passage

The slave trade involved a triangular trade route between Africa, the West Indies, and America. The trade involved ships from New England taking fish to feed slaves in the West Indies, exchanging the fish for molasses, and taking the molasses back to New England to make rum. The rum was taken to the West Coast of Africa, where it was traded for slaves, ivory, and gold dust. The slaves were taken to the West Indies and sold to plantation owners, and the money from their sale was used to buy more molasses.

In Africa, captured men, women, and children were inspected by doctors to ensure their good health, branded like cattle, and packed into ships like sardines in spaces that were often no more than eighteen inches

ALL COLONIES HAD SLAVES

Slavery was not limited to the South, although it was most widespread there. And while every one of the thirteen colonies had a slave system, slavery was not the same in all the colonies. Conditions in the South, where 90 percent of colonial Africans lived, were more severe than in other regions. But even in the South, each colony had its own economy and therefore its own need for slaves. Few slaves lived in the New England colonies, even though New England played a major role in the slave trade. As the New England economy grew, slaves became skilled craftsmen, and some even became doctors.

In the Mid-Atlantic colonies, slavery was more common. Slaves worked on farms and as domestics and craftsmen. Unlike in New England, slave behavior in the Mid-Atlantic colonies was controlled by slave codes that stripped the slaves of most human rights.

MILLIONS BROUGHT FROM AFRICA

While the exact numbers may never be known, the growing demand for labor resulted in an estimated 10-15 million Africans being brought to this country between 1619 and 1807, when Congress passed a law prohibiting participation in the African slave trade. Even after the law was passed, however, other African slaves were smuggled into the country.

The people who made it to America to become slaves were the survivors. An estimated 23 million Africans died before reaching America. Some died in Africa during slave raids, forced marches, and imprisonment in holding cells while waiting for enough "cargo" to fill the ship. Others died of disease in overcrowded ships during the infamous Middle Passage ocean voyage to the West Indies. (This voyage preceded the last leg of their trip to America. In the West Indies, slaves endured a brutal three-month training period known as "seasoning.") Another 17 million may have died in slavery here, bringing the total to 40 million.

high. Some were captured in tribal wars and sold to African slave merchants, who sold them to Europeans. Others were kidnapped by Europeans and Africans. Still others were sold for violating laws. They came from many racial stocks and tribes, and they spoke a variety of languages.

Once on the ship, the captives spent nearly every moment of the next six to ten weeks lying in their tight quarters chained by the neck and legs. They were only taken out on deck to eat and "exercise." The exercise involved jumping around to music played on the fiddle, harp, or bagpipe. Some slaves went crazy before they died. Some, hoping to get enough room to move and breathe, killed the person next to them. Some committed suicide. Some lost the will to live and died. Some tried starving themselves to death. They were often forced to eat with a device containing hot coals to open their mouths. In some cases, their teeth were broken and food was forced down their throats. But the main cause of death was disease. On a typical voyage, one out of eight slaves died. The number was so great that schools of sharks followed the ships from Africa to America, feasting on the dead slaves thrown overboard.

Because of these conditions, slave revolts on board ship were a constant threat. In fact, they were so common that nearly all ship owners bought revolt insurance.

Maintaining Control

Maintaining order in a slave system was not an easy job for slave owners. Just as revolts were a threat on ships, they were a threat throughout the existence of slavery. To help reduce the danger of revolts, slaves were not allowed to talk in their native language. Instead, they had to learn English.

Laws known as slave codes made it illegal to teach a slave to read or write. It was also illegal for slaves to hold meetings (including church services) without a white person present, beat drums, gather in groups of more than two or three when they were not on their home plantation, carry weapons, wear nice clothes, marry or protect their spouses, own anything, or leave the plantation without a written note. Slaves could not defend themselves against whites, and whites could not be convicted of murdering a slave. In addition, a slave could be whipped for standing up straight and looking a white person in the eye.

Punishment — usually in the form of beatings, but also including amputation of limbs, torture, and being sold "down river" to live a harsher life on cotton plantations in the Deep South — was part of daily life for the slave. Some slave owners also used the carrot-and-stick approach to keeping order. In addition to punishing slaves, they might reward those who obeyed by giving them extra food, granting them holidays off, or allowing them to have a dance.

On large plantations, masters also kept order with a highly structured, military-style system in which nearly every activity was controlled. Each day, slaves awoke to the sound of a horn or bell and marched to the fields to begin work as soon as it was light enough to see. Except for a few minutes around noon to eat, slaves worked under the watchful eye of a white overseer and a Black foreman known as a "driver." When it was too dark to see, the slaves were marched back to their quarters, where they fed the livestock, cut wood, and did other chores before they prepared and ate their evening meal. When there was a full moon, the slaves often worked in the field into the middle of the night.

While the military lifestyle certainly helped maintain control, perhaps the most successful means of control was brainwashing, which taught the slaves to hate themselves and fear white people. Brainwashing was a technique that African American historian Carter G. Woodson (who created what is now Black History Month) would later describe as chaining slaves' minds.

Even with brainwashing, the slave owner was not able to squash all rebellion. In big and little ways, slaves learned to rebel against the system. They pretended to be sick and unable to work, pretended not to understand what someone wanted them to do, and "accidentally" broke equipment or destroyed crops. They burned buildings, ran away, and refused, for the most part, to betray another slave to a white person. They killed their masters and the masters' families and planned, attempted, or actually carried out more than two hundred slave revolts and conspiracies.

Slavery Took Many Forms

While the traditional view of slavery centers on life on large plantations, the forms of slavery varied, depending on where the slave lived and worked and on the personality of the slave owner. Some slaves lived in towns, others lived on small family farms, and others lived on large plantations. Some slaves worked as domestics, others as skilled laborers, and others as agricultural workers.

Over half of the four hundred thousand slave owners in 1860 had four or fewer slaves. These slaves usually worked alongside their masters in the fields. While this daily contact may have helped create a more personal relationship between slave and master, these owners were usually poor. This made life harder on the slaves for several reasons. Poor masters could not grow the same amount and variety of food as those on a plantation. They could not replace worn clothing as readily as the plantation master did, and often had to pinch pennies to make ends meet for themselves and their slaves. One other thing made life harder on the slaves of poor masters: They couldn't go to "the quarters" (an area on the plantation where field slaves lived together) to get away from their master's watchful eye at the end of the day.

Working in this environment did not give slaves time to relax. For these reasons, most

Most Africans taken to America worked in agriculture, growing crops such as cotton.

slaves preferred working on larger plantations, where they were generally divided into four groups — the field hands, the domestics, the artisans, and the drivers.

Field Hands. The field hands were housed in a separate area (almost like a military base) called "quarters." Most slaves lived in family-style houses. On a few plantations, these houses were two- or three-room brick structures with windows and a fireplace. On others, home was an army barracks-style building shared by many slaves of all ages. Most houses were one-room log shacks with dirt floors, no windows, and little furniture.

The food plantation slaves ate was very basic and was given to them weekly. Generally, each adult received a peck of corn (roughly sixteen pounds) and three to four pounds of bacon or salt pork a week. Each child received about half that amount. The slaves supplemented their diets by trapping raccoons and opossums or taking corn and chickens from the master's supply.

Their clothing was also very basic. On most plantations, slaves received clothing twice a year. The men usually got two shirts, a pair of wool pants, and a jacket in the fall, and two light-weight shirts and pairs of pants in the spring. Women received wool cloth, buttons, and thread to make cool-weather clothes in the fall, and cotton cloth, buttons, and thread to make spring and summer clothes. Usually once a year, men and women were issued the same kind of shoes — ill-fitting brogans that hurt their feet.

Domestics. Domestics, including butlers, cooks, housemaids, coachmen, and "mammies" who took care of the children, lived either in a wing of the "big house" or in cabins nearby. They slept in beds rather than on the pallets field hands used. They ate better food — often the same as the master — and dressed in uniforms or hand-me-downs from the master's family. Maids and valets often traveled with their master or mistress. Domestic slaves were often taught to read and "spies" passing on information was so great that some whites spelled out words to each other rather than talk normally. House slaves were also known to kill their masters by putting things like arsenic and ground glass in their food.

The Artisans. Skilled laborers included blacksmiths, harness makers, carpenters, and shoemakers. Generally, they were treated better than other slaves and were given more freedom to express themselves. The artisans were chosen from among the other slaves because they were smart and worked well with their hands. Because they had special skills and training and made and repaired much of the equipment needed to run the plantation, artisans were considered valuable. For this reason, the master was less likely to mistreat them. In fact, the master generally allowed them to get away with saying and doing things another slave might be whipped for, such as answering back or disagreeing with the master.

The Drivers. The slave with possibly the most power on the plantation was the driver. He was a trusted individual who, in exchange for special privileges and food, was responsible for maintaining order among the other slaves in the field and the quarters. He made sure they worked and did not slack off, punished improper behavior by the slaves, and reported to the master any problems with the overseer. For the most part, the driver was not a popular person among the other slaves. He became a man caught between two worlds: the world of the master, where he was not fully accepted, and the world of the slave, where he was not trusted.

Some drivers let their power and privilege go to their head and drove the other slaves hard. In some instances, they were killed by

On the larger plantations, slave women played a major role in rearing the slave owner's children.

write, even though this was illegal. For the most part, these workers were children of the master or had light complexions.

Masters tried, to some extent successfully, to separate house and field slaves. House slaves were discouraged from getting together with field slaves and were encouraged to identify with the master. In reality, there was interaction between house and field slaves.

Slave narratives tell of house slaves going to the quarters and entertaining the field slaves with stories about the master and mistress — complete with impersonations. Some house slaves took food from the big house and sent it to the quarters. Others passed on information about things that were discussed by the master or mistress. The concern about fellow slaves. Other drivers tried to make life easier for the slaves without jeopardizing their own positions.

Perhaps the most fortunate slaves were those who lived in urban areas. Most of these slaves worked as domestics and skilled laborers. The skilled laborers were free to hire out their services and earn money that allowed them to purchase their freedom. In addition, urban slaves were able to mix and mingle with free people of color in churches and at social events, which allowed them to develop a greater sense of self-confidence. This self-confidence was reflected in the way they carried themselves — holding their heads up rather than looking down.

After the slave trade was banned by Congress, hiring slaves out became a common practice throughout the South — especially in areas with a surplus of slaves. Brokers matched owners with slaves for hire with those in need of slaves. The terms could be for a day, week, month, or year. Slaves were usually hired for a specific project, and they commonly worked in the iron, coal, hemp, and tobacco industries. Doctors, lawyers, and other professional people also hired slaves as domestics.

Slavery's Impact on the Family

Starting and maintaining a family were difficult for a slave. The legal system did not acknowledge slave marriages. As a result, the owner could and often did sell men, women, and children to different buyers without regard to the impact on the family.

The invention of the cotton gin by Eli Whitney played a major role in breaking up families. The cotton gin, which made separating the seeds from the cotton fiber easier, helped create a boom in the U.S. cotton industry. This resulted in a growing need for slaves in the Deep South and a growing business for whites in the slave-auction business. Perhaps the main slave market city was New Orleans, with its two hundred auction marts, slave showrooms, and show windows where owners could find any type of slave they wanted. Slaves were also bred like horses or dogs to produce the best "stock."

Even under these conditions, many stable marriages and families survived slavery. Many slaves symbolized their marriage to each other by "jumping the broom" (jumping over a broomstick while holding each other's arm). When husbands and wives were sold away from each other, it was common for the husband to run away from the plantation in search of his spouse and children. After emancipation, southern roads were filled with men looking for their wives and children.

Survival Through Community Support

One of the most remarkable feats that emerged out of slavery was not only African Americans' physical survival, but also their emotional and cultural survival. Part of the reason for this was the slaves' ability to create an environment that brought civilization to an uncivilized situation.

Within slave society, there were rules for behavior toward one another and for interaction with the whites. There were also methods for expressing the old cultural ways and developing new ones. One rule of behavior in slave society was respect for elders. Young people were required to use the titles "Auntie" or "Uncle" when speaking to an older person. Another rule was the use of good manners. People of all ages were expected to say "thank you" when someone did them a favor.

The slave community also worked cooperatively to ensure the well-being of its members. Because slave mothers usually had little time to rear their children, that job was left to an older slave woman who took care of children below the age of six in a "children's house." When the children reached six or seven, they went to the fields to help with tasks like carrying water and removing stones. Once they reached the age of ten, eleven, or twelve, they became full-fledged field workers. On some plantations, one group cooked the noon meal for all the workers in the quarter. When it was time to eat, the food was carried out into the field. Each household cooked its own evening meal.

A dual system of morality existed in the slave community. It was all right to take something that belonged to the master, but it was not all right to steal from another slave. It was all right to lie to the master, but it was not all right to betray a fellow slave. This system of dual morality helped slaves get what they needed to survive and resist the forces that were trying to tear their world apart.

Survival for slaves also depended on their ability to mislead whites. It was important to make whites think that the slaves were cooperating or in agreement, even when they were not. Showing a false self to whites is what poet Langston Hughes described years later as wearing the mask. The ability to outwit whites was passed from generation to generation by word and example.

Wearing the mask was also reflected in the leaders and heroes slaves chose. The woman who talked back and got away with it, the man the overseer was afraid to whip, the slave who successfully escaped "up North" — all were heroes in the community, although no one would admit this to a white person.

Finally, slaves survived by creating a spiritual and cultural environment that allowed them to recharge their batteries. Slaves took

the white man's religion, in which he stressed obedience, and turned it into a revolutionary force. Religion became the basis for resisting and fighting the institution of slavery and later segregation and discrimination, and it became a way to relieve the tension and destructive power created by slavery itself.

The slaves also took the few moments of leisure they had on Saturday nights and holidays to dance and have a good time. In these ways, they maintained a balance in a world that would otherwise have thrown their lives into turmoil.

Free People of Color

As indicated earlier, not all Africans were slaves. From the beginning, free people of color lived in this country. Some of them (like the twenty who arrived in 1619) were indentured servants who gained their freedom after they completed their service time. Some gained their freedom by running away from their masters. Some were freed as a reward for serving in colonial wars and the Revolutionary War. Some were set free by their slave master fathers. Some were informally set free by masters who were trying to get around a law that required freed slaves to leave the state immediately. Some purchased their freedom by hiring themselves out to make money. And some lived in territories that later were admitted to the Union.

These free people of color presented a problem — particularly in the South. Their existence gave "ideas" to slaves, making it more difficult to keep slaves in their place. The revolution in Haiti in 1791 and various slave revolts and conspiracies to rebel added to the belief that these free African Americans were a threat.

To protect its interests, the South passed laws to control free African Americans. One

Agriculture was still the primary form of work after slavery. Many former slaves became sharecroppers — paying "rent" on land by giving the landlord part of their crop.

such law said people with dark skin had to prove they were not a slaves. For this reason, free people of color always carried "free papers" issued by the courts. Sometimes even this was not enough to protect them, and slave traders still captured and sold them.

While such a free person could make contracts and own property, he could not hold public office, vote in most states, or testify against white people in most states. Even so, some African Americans living in the South became wealthy and even owned their own slaves.

Unlike their white counterparts, however, these people were not usually motivated by profit. Often, relatives or friends were bought to protect them from the law requiring all freed slaves to leave the state at once. Free people of color also formed benevolent societies to help members and their families during illness and death.

In the North, free African Americans had fewer restrictions on their lives, but still there were some. Some states either forbade or restricted their voting rights. Others would not allow them to testify against white people. Others required them to post a cash bond before they entered the state. Indiana would not allow any free person of color to move to the state to live.

Northern white workers saw freedmen as a threat because many had skills they learned as slaves. Generally, free African Americans were limited to jobs as unskilled workers or domestics. Even so, some managed to make a good living — especially those who started their own businesses. Despite African Americans' successes and efforts to be good citizens, many white settlers tried a number of times to get them to "return" to Africa. Most free African Americans rejected this idea, choosing to make their way in this country.

The extended family is a tradition among African Americans that
mirrors the structure of families in the West African homeland.

CHAPTER THREE

FAMILY AND COMMUNITY
AUNT FREDDIE'S SISTER'S CHILD TWICE REMOVED

Among European Americans, say "family" and generally a father, mother, and children pop to mind. But among African Americans, "family" usually brings to mind thoughts of grandparents, aunts, uncles, cousins, and sometimes people who aren't even related. Often these "real" relatives and "play" relatives may not live in the same house, but they are considered part of the family's inner circle.

The extended family, as this is called, has its roots in West African culture. Traditional African families are organized around a core of related people and those who marry into the family. In more rural communities, the family group lives together in a compound where all of the children consider themselves brothers and sisters. It is through this extended family system that the economic, social, educational, disciplinary, and emotional needs of individual people *and* the community are met.

Blood Is Thicker than Water

In West African culture, blood ties are considered more lasting and more important than any other — even more important than marriage. As a result, children of broken marriages may stay in the village of their birth, choosing to live with relatives rather than follow a parent who is moving back to *her or his* home village.

Marriage is seen as the union of two families, not just of two people. Each family group expands to include the other. From that point on, the members of both families consider themselves to be relatives. The idea of marriage as the bringing together of two families is common among various ethnic American communities. But along with the importance of blood ties, the "marriage" of families is especially pronounced in African American culture, where someone is likely to introduce a person as "my sister Judy by marriage." Even after divorce, African Americans often think of members of their ex-spouse's family as relatives.

Children Are Important

Like the value of blood ties, the cherished role of children in African American families can also be traced to African culture, where

The African proverb "it takes a whole village to raise a child" reflects the central role children play in traditional West African and African American families.

each adult is expected to help guide the development of all children in the family — no matter who the parents are. An African proverb, "it takes a whole village to raise a child," reflects the central importance of children and the duty of adults. Motherhood is also highly regarded in African culture. A son is expected not only to obey his mother, but to demonstrate his love and devotion to her.

Many other family values are held in high regard in African culture. These include showing reverence and respect for elders and cooperation in getting work done, without regard to whether the work is "men's work," "women's work," or "children's work." African culture also teaches the importance of taking responsibility for the well-being of others by maintaining a balance among the rights of the individual, the needs of the family and larger group, and the rights of others beyond the group.

African Family Values Continue in America

While urban living and hundreds of years of Western European influence have had an impact, these African values still run through

African American culture. As we have seen, the importance placed on blood ties is one sign of the respect African Americans have for people within their extended family and community. In addition to using the common expression "blood is thicker than water," African Americans use the words "brother," "sister," and "blood" to describe a person who shares a common African ancestry. Blood ties are also reflected in how often African American relatives (and even unrelated people) will rear children without formally adopting them or serve as their foster parents. Blood ties also extend to the grief African Americans feel over the deaths of people within and beyond the immediate family.

When ministers in African American churches announce the names of people who have asked others to pray on their behalf, it is not unusual to hear a request from someone who is bereaved because a distant relative, such as an older aunt or uncle, has died. Nor is it unusual for African Americans to travel long distances to attend the funeral of a distant relative.

The idea of the extended African American family also has an effect on notions of

KWANZA: A MODERN AFRICAN AMERICAN TRADITION

In 1966, civil rights activist Maulan Ron Karenga developed an idea for a holiday that would be specifically for African Americans. The holiday is called Kwanza — Swahili for "first fruits." It was created to remind African Americans of their traditional values and to teach those values to the next generation.

The values that are highlighted during this holiday, which runs for seven days beginning on December 26, reflect the

traditional values of African culture and family:

1. *Umoja* — unity
2. *Kujichaguila* — self-determination
3. *Ugima* — collective work and responsibility
4. *Ujamaa* — cooperative economics
5. *Nia* — purpose
6. *Kuumba* — creativity
7. *Imani* — faith

hospitality and inconvenience. When people move to a town where they have a relative — even a distant relative — it would be unusual for them not to stay with that relative while they are looking for a permanent place to live. Whether or not such a visit would be "inconvenient" for the relative is less important than helping out a member of the family.

The Family as Teacher

In addition to making family members feel comfortable and respected, the family in African American society plays another critical role — teacher.

The family teaches its members to overcome negative social attitudes and acts that may hurt their self-esteem. The family provides young people with guidelines for coping with new or confusing situations, becoming independent and self-reliant, and responding quickly to change. It also helps young people learn how to form positive friendships in the African American community — and how to survive with dignity as part of both the African and European American cultures.

This might mean helping a son overcome a hurtful act of name-calling, or boosting the self-confidence of a daughter whose teacher has advised her not to take a class because it might be too "hard" for her. Or it might mean learning how to counteract the assumption by members of other ethnic groups that a gathering of young African American males talking on a street corner must belong to a gang.

Tough Love

Because African American parents know the difficulties their children will face, many favor the "tough love" approach to rearing their kids. This approach — which emphasizes discipline and obedience — is considered a sign of love and a way to make life easier for children by helping them develop the qualities that are important to African American survival and success: a commitment to family and education; cooperation for economic, political and social goals; self-governance; service; hard work; moral and ethical behavior; and racial pride.

Parents who practice "tough love" expect an immediate response to commands and do not tolerate tantrums, dirty looks, or pouting. While this approach may involve spankings, this is not the only method used. Discipline and obedience can be instilled by using verbal warnings — "you're about to get on my last nerve"; "don't you look at me in that tone of voice" — or with a nonverbal form of communication known as "the look." This nonverbal warning, which is practiced primarily by African American mothers, lets children know in no uncertain terms that they have now reached the limits of acceptable behavior.

Everyone Is a Relative

The idea of the extended family surfaces in African American culture in many ways, some of them more subtle than others: Because most African Americans consider themselves "brothers and sisters" based on their shared ancestry, the accomplishments or mistakes of one person are often viewed as reflecting on everyone. When Joe Louis and Muhammad Ali won and lost the heavyweight boxing title, millions of African Americans felt *they* had won and lost. When Jackie Robinson became the first African American to play in the modern major leagues, millions of African Americans felt *they* had broken the barriers of segregation and made it into the majors.

When quarterback Doug Williams returned to the field after suffering what looked like a game-ending leg injury during Super Bowl XXII — and went on to lead his team to victory, set or tie several Super Bowl records, and earn the MVP award — millions of African Americans felt *they* had earned the right to go to Disney World. When Vanessa Williams was crowned the first African American Miss America, millions of African Americans felt a sense of joy at the crumbling of this barrier to recognizing that Black was also beautiful. And when her crown was taken away after the publication of photographs that were not in keeping with Miss America's image, millions of African Americans felt *they* had lost the crown.

There's No One Like Mamma

One African value that not only survived slavery but has persisted in African American culture is the respect for mothers. One of the fastest ways to start an argument or a fight particularly with an African American male, is to say something negative about someone's mother. Other members of the family may be fair game, but mothers are off-limits. When athletes look into the camera and send greetings home, it's always "Hi, mom." This does not mean fathers are not considered important. Rather, it reflects the African tradition of honoring the one who brings life into the world — a tradition that was strengthened during slavery when the mother became the glue that held everyone together and main-

A victory for one is a victory for all. *Left:* Former Washington quarterback Doug Williams made African Americans swell with pride after his record-setting performance in Super Bowl XXII. *Right:* Vanessa Williams was the first African American crowned Miss America.

tained a sense of family when its members were sold to other plantations.

Reaching Back

Yet another key African American value rooted in the culture of the homeland is the belief that those who achieve success have a duty to help others. For this reason, one measure of an African American politician's success is whether he or she looks out for the interests of African Americans. Those who have — such as Representative Adam Clayton Powell, Jr., Rev. Jesse Jackson, and Senator Carol Moseley-Braun — earn the support of the people. In some instances (as was the case with former Washington, D.C., mayor Marion Barry, who was convicted of drug use), some African Americans even support a politician whose behavior does not follow the straight and narrow if that politician has "taken care of business for the people."

Young people who succeed in life are expected to help out other family members. This assistance could come in the form of putting a brother or sister through school, helping a parent pay bills or buy a home, or stepping in to help solve family problems and disputes.

Within the African American community, growing numbers of athletes, entertain-

Top: Senator Carol Moseley-Braun — the first African American woman elected to the U.S. Senate.
Bottom: Reaching back to help others is part of the tradition in African American culture. Rev. Jesse Jackson — founder and head of Operation PUSH and the Rainbow Coalition — and talk show host Oprah Winfrey work to improve the lives of African Americans.

ers, and business people are contributing time and money to help solve some of the social ills affecting urban centers in this country. These

African American women have worked outside the home for centuries.

people include athletes and entertainers such as Green Bay Packers defensive end Reggie White, Phoenix Suns guard Kevin Johnson, comedian Bill Cosby, and talk show host Oprah Winfrey.

This list also includes such business people as the late Reginald Lewis, who headed an international food processing and distribution company that is the nation's largest African American-owned business, and Ed Gardner, who owns the country's largest African American-owned hair care products manufacturing company and the nation's largest African American-owned theater for producing plays.

The sense that there is a need to "give back" is not limited to athletes, entertainers, or successful business people. It is a thread woven throughout the fabric of African American culture. Fraternities and sororities are not merely social organizations, they also get involved in activities designed to help improve the lives of others in the African American community. These activities might include raising money for scholarships, presenting awards that recognize individuals for their contributions to the community, sponsoring contests to showcase young talent, and even posting rewards to assist in the capture of criminals.

Paying Homage to the Ancestors

Respect for elders is another value handed down from the African homeland. Older women in the church are referred to as "mothers of the church" and are accorded special status and respect. More and more African American events open with ceremonies or statements recognizing the contributions of the "ancestors" and giving honor to the "elders" of the community. At family reunions, recognition is given to the senior member of the family, and growing numbers of African Americans are tracing their roots to learn more about the people on whose "shoulders" they stand.

Equal Rights

One final characteristic of the African American family that is rooted in African tradition is shared responsibility. Historically, African American women have had more freedom to take part in the decision-making process in the family. The foundation for this freedom is in African society, where titles, rights, and property were passed from one generation to another along kinship lines. That meant that husbands could not control their wives' property. In America, this pattern continued during slavery and segregation because women often had to assume responsibility for providing for the family when their husbands were sold to another plantation or were unable to find employment.

Working together and sharing responsibility is part of the family tradition.

Working Together for Family Survival

The wages earned solely by a working father have usually not been enough to support his entire family. So while two-income families are common in the United States today, the economic survival of the African American family has long depended on having a second income. Working outside of the home has been commonplace for African American women since the first Africans came to America.

In fact, most African American females are taught that they will probably have to contribute to the support of their family. Many are also taught that "every tub has to sit on its own bottom" — meaning they must prepare to support themselves because they may not find a husband.

Even for African American families that are not struggling financially, upward mobility and maintaining a middle-class lifestyle depend heavily on having two earners in the family. Most families have reached this point through hard work, not inheritance. What they *have* inherited is a strong work ethic that has given them the tools to survive hard times.

Getting the Job Done

How work gets done in the African American family is another way that shared responsibility is demonstrated. While some activities are considered "men's work," "women's work," and "children's work," the emphasis is not on who does what, but rather on getting the job done. For example, if the parents are away from home, the job of taking care of smaller children rests with the oldest child — regardless of whether that child is a girl or boy. Household chores, yard work, grocery shopping, getting children ready for school, helping children with homework, paying the bills — they may all be done by either sex.

This all-for-one, one-for-all attitude has been the source of strength in the African American community. It is a principal reason for the survival of African Americans and of African American culture in this country despite tremendous hardships and an often hostile environment.

Spirituals and gospel music sung in many African American churches reflect the deep faith that is part of the religious tradition and the key role religion plays in daily life.

CHAPTER FOUR

RELIGION AND CELEBRATIONS
WE'VE COME THIS FAR BY FAITH

"I don't feel no ways tired. I've come too far from where I've started from. Nobody told me that the road would be easy. But, I don't believe He'd bring me this far just to leave me." As the words to this gospel song suggest, faith in God has both comforted and strengthened African Americans, whose lives have been marred by oppression and discrimination throughout their history in this country. That faith prompted unknown slaves to create the religious music called spirituals and develop a style of worship that both expresses feelings and provides a release from the tensions and difficulties of everyday living.

Religious faith is a key part of African American life. In a national survey, 84 percent of African Americans said they consider themselves religious, another 76 percent said religion played an important role in their lives

Expressing feelings during the worship service is part of the tradition in many African American churches. This expression can range from verbal responses such as "amen" or "have mercy" to standing up, clapping, or doing a "holy dance."

when they were growing up, 77 percent said the church still had a major influence in their lives, and 80 percent said it is important to send children to church. About 78 percent of those in the survey also said they prayed daily, and another 71 percent said they attended church regularly.

Today, most African Americans are Christians — most of them Protestant. In 1989, about half of twenty-four million African American Christian church members were Baptist, nearly 20 percent were Methodist, 16 percent were members of the Church of God in Christ, and 8 percent were Catholic.

Let the Church Say "Amen"

Church in the African American community is a participatory activity. Members of the congregation are expected to respond to "the Word" and to the music as the spirit moves them. This means members of the congregation may shout out "preach," "tell it," "have mercy," "amen," or some other expression that lets the preacher, choir, or prayer leader know the members of the congregation have heard, understood, and agree with what is being said. This style of participation, dubbed call and response, is a way of talking back that is rooted in West African traditions of religious observance that include ritual dance, song, and a free display of emotions.

Sometimes the truth of the message becomes so overpowering that a member of the congregation becomes filled with the Holy Ghost — the spirit of God — and "shouts." Shouting may be vocal or silent. In either instance, it involves what anthropologist Zora Neale Hurston described as a state of "possession" in which the Spirit "drive[s] out the individual consciousness temporarily and use[s] the body for its expression."

When a member of the congregation becomes filled with the Holy Ghost — the spirit of God — during a church service, he or she may "shout."

In every case, the person claims ignorance of his or her actions during the possession. During such time, the person may wave his or her arms in the air, stand up, jump, jerk or twitch, do a holy dance, moan and go limp, or become rigid once the spirit has left.

An usher or individual sitting near such people

The rite of baptism is carried out in different ways in different African American churches. Some sprinkle or pour water on people's heads. Others fully immerse them in water. Years ago, full-immersion baptism might take place in a river. Today, most churches use pools.

removes their glasses, fans them, and restrains them enough to keep them from hurting themselves or others, but not so much that they are not free to move in accordance with the will of the Spirit. Shouting is usually contagious. When one person begins to shout, others often do so, too.

The degree to which church members shout may vary from one religious denomination to another and even from church to church within a denomination. Some of the more conservative African American church services closely resemble sober European American church services. However, most African American church services do involve some demonstration of emotions — even if it is a quiet "amen." In some churches, however, a quiet "amen" is not enough. Members of these churches believe they have not "had church" unless the preacher has gotten the congregation to shout.

Eliciting the shout is done by a combination of music and a preaching style that is rhythmic, repetitive, and touches an emotional chord in the congregation. The speaking styles of the Rev. Jesse Jackson or the late Rev. Dr. Martin Luther King, Jr., are more refined examples of this style.

Some ministers use a more highly charged emotional style, humming, moaning, rearing back, acting out their sermons, singing, or talking in a booming voice. However, the preacher need not raise his or her voice to elicit a shout from the congregation. Ministers who speak in conversational tones can also elicit shouts by relating the stories and lessons from the Bible to things that affect the lives of their congregation today.

An Activist Tradition

Faith and the church is more than singing, shouting, and preaching; it is the foundation upon which the liberation of African Americans is built. That faith led people such as Harriet Tubman (known as Moses) to lead hundreds of runaway slaves to the promised land of freedom via the Underground Railroad. It prompted Nat Turner, a minister, to lead a slave revolt that he said God told him to carry out. Faith caused a Hurley, New York, slave named Isabella to change her name to Sojourner Truth and wander the country, speaking out against slavery. It made Richard Allen, a former slave, start the African Methodist Episcopal (A. M. E.) Church after he and others walked out of St. George's Church in Philadelphia in protest in 1787 when they were not allowed to finish praying at the altar.

Faith in God was the moral foundation upon which the civil rights movement of the 1950s and 1960s was built; the walls of segregation came tumbling down amid the sounds of many voices singing spirituals and gospel songs.

Faith in God is also the backbone for a growing effort among African Americans to reclaim their community from gangs, violence, and the poverty that is at the root of these maladies. Clergymen — such as the Rev. Jesse Jackson; the Rev. Benjamin Chavez, president of the NAACP; the Rev. Johnnie Ray Youngblood, whose St. Paul Community Baptist Church is reclaiming its Brooklyn neighborhood; and the Rev. Cecil L. Murray, whose church is doing the same thing in Los Angeles — are among those making a difference in urban communities.

As these examples suggest, religion has a strong activist tradition among African Americans. During slavery and later during segregation, those supporting the idea of white supremacy tried to use passages from the Bible

Youth choirs are common in African American churches. They also perform at festivals and other non-church events.

to justify their positions. But African Americans took that same Bible and drew from it the belief that they, too, would one day be free. Slaves created songs like "Steal Away to Jesus" and "Swing Low, Sweet Chariot" that became signals to runaway slaves that it was time to go to a designated site where they would begin their journey to freedom along the Underground Railroad.

On some plantations, religion became such a threat that owners actually forbade its practice by slaves on the plantation, so they went out into the woods to hold services. Songs such as "Couldn't Hear Nobody Pray" were signals by a lookout that the services had not been detected.

A Key Institution

In keeping with its activist tradition, the church and the minister have also played significant leadership roles in the African American community. Traditionally, this leadership role has not only been religious and moral but also social, cultural, political, economic, and educational. In years past, churches were the center of social activity for young people and adults.

While that role is not as strong today, it still exists. In addition to the usual programs, such as Sunday School, youth choirs, and youth ushers, churches sponsor Girl Scout and Boy Scout troops, little league baseball teams, and activities such as roller skating parties and camping trips as wholesome alternatives to young people. Some churches have also established singles groups for their single members and sponsor cruises, outings to sporting and cultural events, and other activities. Women's Day, Men's Day, and Ushers' and Nurses' Day, in addition to raising money for the church, provide social outlets and give people who might not otherwise have an

Leontyne Price, considered one of the world's greatest sopranos, received her early training by singing in church.

opportunity a chance to serve in leadership roles.

The role of churches in the development of African American music is legendary. In fact, what we call soul music is an outgrowth of the gospel and spiritual songs sung in the African American church. So are jazz and the blues. The church not only has been the launching pad for religious music giants like Mahalia Jackson, but it also helped launch the careers of opera singers like Marian Anderson and Leontyne Price, pop singers such as Whitney Houston, and rhythm and blues singers like Aretha Franklin.

African American churches have also nurtured theater and the dramatic arts. Many churches put on plays through their Sunday

Aretha Franklin received the titled "Queen of Soul" because of her gospel-influenced singing style.

School department or drama guild for Christmas, Easter, Mother's Day, Father's Day, and other special occasions.

Some of these are original works written by a member of the congregation. In some churches, playwrights have written nonreligious plays that are presented in the church hall.

Political Power. Churches have also been a source of political power in the African American community. This power is frequently recognized during election time, when candidates running for office visit African American churches seeking support from the members of the congregation. In addition, in just about any community with a significant African American population, pastors of large congregations and organizations of African American clergy have access to elected offi-

cials to advocate for issues that affect the African American community. One legendary congregation is the Abyssinian Baptist Church in Harlem, which also produced one of this century's most powerful African American politicians — Representative Adam Clayton Powell, Jr. — the pastor of that church.

Churches have also been the base of operation for voter registration and get-out-the-vote drives. During the civil rights campaigns of the 1950s and 1960s, African American churches often were meeting places for organizing and putting out information during desegregation struggles in the South. The First A. M. E. Church in Los Angeles was a focal point of activities following the riots after the first verdict in the Rodney King beating case. The church has also been involved in efforts to rebuild that city.

This brings up the next role of the African American church — economic development. Perhaps no other African American-directed institution controls more money than the African American church. In addition to controlling and handling a significant amount of money, African American churches deposit millions of dollars in banks around the country.

Money: A Tradition of Self-Help. Church involvement in economic development is not something new. As far back as slavery, African American churches were involved in economic, political, and social activities to help members of their congregation.

A growing number of African American churches today are following in this tradition of economic self-help by playing a significant role in the revitalization of African American communities. The Rev. T. J. Jemison, president of the National Baptist Convention U.S.A. — the largest African American de-

Politicians recognize the political power and influence of the church in the African American community. Bill Clinton visited the Allen A. M. E. church in Washington, D.C., and read to children during his campaign for the presidency.

nomination — told a convention of delegates in 1991 that the top priority of the church would be to restore the black family to its position of strength, in part by selling "everything black people use."

African American churches in cities and small communities around the country rehabilitate housing, make business loans, own shopping malls and fast food franchises that provide jobs for people in the community, and own apartment buildings, senior citizen homes, auto repair shops, restaurants, and food processing plants. These churches are helping provide the economic clout needed by African American communities.

While these business are run in a professional way, the work of economic development is viewed as part of the mission of the church — to feed the hungry, clothe the naked, and minister to the needs of the least

of these. Once again, this demonstrates the role of the African American church as not only a spiritual institution but also as a force for social change.

The Church and Education

Just as economic development is part of the mission of the church, so, too, is education. African American churches have been involved in the education of African American people for centuries. During the early years, the Bible was the textbook people used when learning to read. Following the Emancipation Proclamation, African American congregations built schools to help educate the newly freed slaves. Education became a much sought-after prize because it was seen as the first step on the road to equality. So churches encouraged young people in whatever way they could to excel academically.

One tool was the oratorical contest. The contests, in which young people memorized famous speeches or wrote and presented speeches on a designated topic, have long been used by churches to help teach speaking and presentation skills. Some students have won prize money through these contests that has helped pay for their education.

On a less competitive level, young people are taught Bible verses in Sunday School, which they then recite in front of the congregation or at a special assembly. Again, this activity is meant to help sharpen youngsters' speaking skills.

The Growth of Islam Among African Americans

While most African Americans are Christians, a growing number are Muslim. The growth of Islam in this country began before World War II, fueled by the creation of the Nation of Islam by W. D. Fard in Detroit in the 1930s. After World War II, thousands of Muslims from Africa and Asia emigrated to the United States.

Today, an estimated 252,000 Muslims in America are African American. In addition to membership in the Nation of Islam, these African Americans are members of the Sunni and Shiite sects.

Part of the reason for this growth is an increasing interest in renewing ties to the African homeland; many Africans brought to this country as slaves were Muslim. In addition, some converts to Islam did so because they saw Christianity as the slave master's religion. Others cited the appeal of Islam's focus on pride, self-respect, respect for others, self-reliance, discipline, morality, and self-defense. The religion is also viewed by some as more straightforward and easier to understand than Christianity.

The African American Tradition in Folklore

Understanding the religious beliefs and practices of a group of people is one way to learn about the core values that guide their lives. Another way is to understand their folklore, legends, stories, and superstitions.

African American folktales and stories developed out of the oral culture of West Africa. The key person in this oral culture is the griot (gree-O), who is both the historian and the educator for his community. His job is to remember and recite the story of his people from the beginning of time. This recitation includes information about who the ancestors of each family are and facts about their lives. It was a griot who helped *Roots* author Alex Haley confirm that Kunta Kinte was his great-great-great-great-great grandfather. To confirm this, the griot had to recite two hundred years of history. In addition to these roles, the griot served as the adviser and confidant to the king and kept people informed about their proper roles in traditional African society.

Because most slave masters would not allow their slaves to learn to read and write (in fact, some states passed laws against this), the African oral storytelling tradition continued in America. While many of the core values of West African culture that were reflected in stories and folk traditions survived the trip from Africa to America, the brutal conditions of slavery created subtle changes in the stories that became part of the African American folk tradition.

One of the characters used most in African American stories is the animal trickster. The main trickster is Brer Rabbit. The rabbit, like the hare in African tales, is used because it is a creature that uses its wits and brain to survive among larger, more powerful animals.

In African American stories, the rabbit uses disguises and cunning to get others to do his work. It is not too hard to understand the message behind the story. It reflects the slaves' wish to get away from their harsh environment of forced labor. Telling and retelling the stories in their many variations was a way for the slave to rebel that did not put him or her in danger of punishment. These animal tricksters and human tricksters became heroes to people facing oppression every day.

"I'll Fly Away"

Another common theme in African American stories is escape. Stories featuring people who could fly are a common part of the African American folklore tradition. Nobel Prize-winning writer Toni Morrison included a person who could fly in her book *Song of Solomon*.

A modern-day storyteller continues a tradition rooted in West African culture.

One of the most famous escape stories is about the Ibo people. The Ibo Landing legend recounts how a group of eighteen Ibo adults were tricked into sailing to America to "work." When they arrived at St. Simon's Island on the coast of Georgia, they discovered the real plan was to sell them into slavery. The Ibo decided they would rather die than live as slaves. They chained themselves together and walked backward into Dunbar Creek, singing a song in their native language as they walked to their death. Legend says that on certain moonlight nights, their voices and clinking chains can still be heard.

Humor is another characteristic of African American folklore. The humor often pokes fun at situations that are not funny — the clothes people had to wear, the food they had to eat. During slavery, they also poked fun at the master and his family. It is all part of the tradition poet Langston Hughes called "laughing to keep from crying." This tradi-

Traditional African American humor not only makes people laugh at things that are funny, but also turns things that may not be funny (like having to wear hand-me-down clothes) into funny stories. Humorous stories about growing up with his brother Russell helped launch the career of comedian Bill Cosby.

tion of wit and humor is carried on by comedians like Will Smith, Sinbad, and Bill Cosby.

West African Religious Beliefs

The belief in supernatural beings, another theme in African American folk tradition, came to America with the slaves. In traditional West African religious belief, a supreme god created the universe and the laws that control nature and human behavior. This god did not get involved in people's day-to-day lives, although the spirits of dead relatives helped tie the living to their god — providing the living led righteous lives and honored their dead ancestors.

Traditional West African religion also held that all things — living and inanimate — have being or spirit. Their god was believed to live in or visit certain rivers, trees,

mountains, and rocks, and sometimes it appeared in human form — particularly in a dream. While belief in this kind of supernatural world is not common among most African Americans today, some parts of this belief system continue among some. Practicing the religion of Voodoo (ancestor worship) still occurs in some parts of the country. Even among those who don't practice Voodoo, the suggestion that someone might "work roots" (cast a spell) can make them uncomfortable and nervous.

Certain superstitions that developed early in African American history also continue to exist among some people. For example: If your palms itch, you will receive money. If your ears ring, someone is talking about you. If you place your purse on the floor, you will lose money. If you cut your hair when the moon is wasting, it will break off; but if you cut it when the moon is growing, your hair will grow.

These superstitions reflect the relationship African Americans feel between themselves and all other beings and things on earth. Superstitions are a worldly reflection of the West African sacred belief system that says all things in the universe are connected and affect each other.

The same belief in the relationship between all things is found in African American religion. Faith among African Americans is not isolated from everyday life. It is at the core of life and, as such, has been the foundation upon which the liberation of African Americans has been based. The African American church — probably the strongest institution in the African American community — continues to play a role in helping the community deal with economic development and political, social, and educational issues.

Voodoo is rooted in the ancestor worship of traditional West African religion.

THE IBO LANDING SONG

Oh freedom, oh freedom, oh freedom over me
And before I'd be a slave I'll be buried in my grave
And go home to my Lord and be free.
No more crying, no more crying, no more crying will there be
And before I'd be a slave I'll be buried in my grave
And go home to my Lord and be free.
No more groaning, no more dying will there be
And before I'd be a slave I'll be buried in my grave
And go home to my Lord and be free.
Oh freedom, oh freedom, oh freedom over me
And before I'd be a slave I'll be buried in my grave
And go home to my Lord and be free.

A creative combination: an outfit that is African from the neck
up, American from the neck down.

CHAPTER FIVE

CUSTOMS, EXPRESSIONS, AND HOSPITALITY
STYLE POINTS

"**I**t ain't what you do, it's the way you do it." This line, sung by Johnnie Taylor in the 1970s, makes a point about African American culture — style is important. Whether it's Michael "Air" Jordan creating a new way to put the ball in the hoop, or Will making crushing remarks about his preppie cousin Carleton on the television show "Fresh Prince of Bel-Air," or the musical group Kris Kross wearing their pants backwards, style counts.

Style is a way to make a statement about yourself — who you are and what makes you different from everyone else in the universe. It is a way to stake out your place in the world.

To be genuine, style must be cool, smooth, and unpretentious — something you just naturally have, not an image you work hard to create. As with much of African American culture, the roots of cool lie deep in West African culture. The concept of what is called "cool" is believed to have started among royalty in Nigeria around 2000-3000 B.C. The cool pose is rooted in the belief that to have *ashe* (pronounced ah-SHAY) — an inner spirituality, peace, strength, sophistication, nobility, and control — is the mark of a truly whole person.

Language: Rappin' and Signifyin'

Language in African American culture is often used in colorful and original ways. In fact, many words and phrases that are now part of American English made their way into the popular culture from African American culture. One phrase, "the real McCoy," was created to describe a device invented by Elijah McCoy, the son of former slaves. McCoy's invention automatically oiled machinery while the machine was running. The device worked so well that people shopping for manufacturing equipment would ask whether the machinery was equipped with "the real McCoy."

Even though African American slang and phrases are becoming part of everyday speech and hip-hop culture is blurring the lines between the way young African Americans and young people of other cultures speak, African American speech is still like a foreign language to many non-African Americans. Looked at this way, most African Americans can speak two languages — "Black English" and "standard English." For example, a person talking to his or her "partners" (friends) may greet them by saying "What's up?" When talking to someone who is not African American, that greeting may become "Hello" or "Hi."

Boasting and hyperbole (an exaggerated claim) are other features of the way African Americans speak. After his fights, former heavy weight champion Muhammad Ali would brag that his opponent never touched him. As proof, Ali would stroke his face and say "I'm still pretty."

While his style of speech was different from that of Dr. King, Malcolm X could also move people to challenge inequality in America and stand up for their rights.

The Rev. Dr. Martin Luther King, Jr., was a skilled orator whose ability to move people with his words and voice grew out of the Black Baptist preaching style.

Another feature of African American speech rooted in West African culture is the use of humor, wit, and emotion. Clever, sometimes biting comments are used to show intelligence and mental quickness while also revealing something about the speaker's personality. Muhammad Ali in his prime spoke in rhyme. The Rev. Dr. Martin Luther King, Jr., took people to the mountain top to view his dream with just his words and his voice. Malcolm X, while appearing cool and controlled outside, issued fiery challenges to racial inequality in America.

African American verbal skills have actually become an art form called "the dozens" (also known as signifyin' and joning) — a verbal duel in which people make insulting remarks about each other and their families. The duel requires each person to keep his or her emotions under control, think quickly, and come back with an even more cutting remark. A typical duel might include an exchange like this:

First person: "Your sister so ugly, she got to sneak up on a mirror in the morning to get a look at herself."

Second person: "Well, your sister so ugly they passed a law against her coming outside *without* a Halloween mask on."

"Woofing" or "selling woof tickets" is another form of verbal challenge — this time one that threatens action. But, as is the case with the boy who cried "woof," the threat is generally considered all talk and no action.

This kind of high-powered joking is a common part of a card game popular among

African Americans — bid whist. A player, knowing full well he or she is outmatched in the game, might say something like "come on with it. I got something for you," as he or she waves a card in the air, preparing to slam it on the table. The ploy is used to make opponents change their mind about the card they were planning to play. If successful, the ploy could help the bluffing player and his partner win that hand in the card game.

Dramatic Arguing

African American culture also allows for greater freedom in the way a person expresses his or her ideas, feelings, and beliefs. You can be dramatic (using your hands and body to emphasize or act out what you're saying), emotional, make personal comments, and argue your point forcefully — all without losing your temper. When debating an issue in African American culture, you are not just trying to show off your debating skills. You are trying to convince someone that your point of view is right. Therefore, you are expected to argue strongly in favor of your position. Doing so shows you care enough about your position to put real effort behind winning the other person over to your point of view.

Arguing forcefully for an idea is also a way to determine what the "truth" is. During a debate, if a person does not come back with a strong statement opposing something you say, it is assumed he or she agrees with you.

The more times a person "agrees" with his or her opponent's comments, the weaker his or her position becomes. The person who wins a debate is generally the one who out-thinks, out-talks (even interrupting), and is more clever in the way he or she presents a position.

To someone not familiar with this style, what an African American considers to be a debate may appear to be a heated argument. In reality, the danger of conflict, including physical conflict, increases when the talking actually stops.

Nonverbal Communication

Body language is also an important part of communication. Conversations may be punctuated not only with hand movements, but also with body movements as the speaker tells *and* acts out a story.

Body language also includes attitudes about personal space. In African American culture, getting too close to someone's face uninvited, known as "getting in someone's face," or pointing a finger in a person's face could be considered a hostile act and lead to an argument or fight. Entering this personal space uninvited — especially if an argument is taking place — is considered a signal that a physical attack is about to occur.

Eye contact is also a part of body language. Like other racial and ethnic groups, Africans largely adapted to "American" culture. But not completely. In African cultures, looking directly into someone's eyes for too long is not polite. This belief and tradition still exists, to a large extent, in African American culture. That is why many African Americans will look away occasionally as they talk to someone.

Stylin' 'n' Profilin'

Dress among African Americans is more than a way to cover or protect the body; it is a way to make a personal statement about who you are and what you are like. Dress can affect what others think about your status in life and how much power you have. Even if you are a successful or wealthy person, if you don't dress the part, others will not think of you in those terms. Dressing the part means wearing stylish, expensive-looking clothes, and being "clean," sharply dressed, whenever you are out in public.

Being creative or original in dress is admired in African American culture. Wearing unlaced sneakers, pants on backwards, bib overalls with one side unbuttoned, multiple earrings in one ear, fingernails painted multiple colors and decorated with rhinestones, hair braided in fancy styles, dredlocks, complicated designs cut into men's hair, gold chains, and kofia hats (round cloth hats without brims) all are part of creative African American dress.

Creativity and originality are also seen in the choice of colors. Generally, African Ameri-

cans prefer bright colors — perhaps reflecting the colors found in their ancestors' countries. And these colors are often mixed and matched in ways that break the rules about what colors look good together — for example, red and green, yellow and red, purple and green.

During the Harlem Renaissance of the 1920s — a period when African American art and artists were popular and influenced other artists in this country — one of the most talented and respected poets, Langston Hughes, wrote several poems that reflect pride and appreciation for color. Two of these poems are "Color" and "When Susanna Jones Wears Red." In "Color," Hughes instructs his reader to wear color "Like a banner / For the proud — / Not like a shroud," and to "Wear it / Like a song / Soaring high — / Not moan or cry."

Bright colors, stylish clothes, and creative or original ways of dressing are part of African Americans' "style."

Changing Fashions

African Americans' style of dress and use of color have influenced fashion, not only in America but also worldwide. As late as the 1960s, European American men were clean-shaven and were still wearing white shirts (hence, the phrase white-collar worker) with dark suits and conservative ties. European American women wore button-style earrings. European Americans with curly hair ironed it, rolled it up on tin cans, or looked for other ways to straighten it out. The Black revolution of the 1960s, with its emphasis on Black pride and things African, led African American women to start wearing large hoop

and dangle earrings and piercing their ears. The "natural" (also called the Afro) hairdo was worn by men and women, and some (such as actress Cicely Tyson) began to have their hair braided.

Braided hair caused conflict in the 1970s. Some African American women were fired or disciplined for wearing their hair in braids and refusing to change the style. Companies defended their action by saying the hairstyle did not fit the image they wanted their employees to project to their customers. When

More African Americans are wearing traditional African clothing and styles based on this traditional clothing. Their talent for mixing Western and African styles has influenced the way people from other ethnic groups dress.

Above: Braided hair is a West African style that has become popular among African Americans. *Right:* The Jackson 5 influenced not only pop music, but also the way many non-African American pop singers dressed.

the European American movie star Bo Derek appeared in the film *10* wearing braids, the style became acceptable. Many African Americans were offended that the style they had introduced was not considered acceptable until someone from the dominant culture made it so.

Facial hair for men, which has always been fairly common in African American culture, took on another dimension in the 1960s. Instead of just growing a mustache, more African American men began growing beards. African styles and clothes made from African material grew in popularity among African Americans during the 1960s, and the trend was reflected more and more in clothes developed by the world's fashion designers. "Jungle prints," bright colors and styles that reflected African dress, began to grow in popularity in the U.S.

Influenced by such films as *Superfly* and *Shaft,* the clothing worn by African American males in the 1970s took on a more colorful, urban look. The clothing included platform shoes with wide, high heels, bell-bottom pants, wide-brimmed hats, and bright colors. This look also had an impact on the general American culture. Even among European American corporate types, white shirts gave way to colored and striped shirts. Conservative ties became more colorful. Men wore gold necklaces and bracelets as part of their casual look. The change was dubbed the "peacock revolution."

Fashion today continues to be influenced by African Americans. Colorful clothes are the norm. New fashion trends — particularly among young people — often start in urban African American culture. Hip-hop dress, the clothing style originated by young African Americans who live in the central city, is loose fitting, casual, and colorful. The dress is part of a larger hip-hop culture that moves to a rap music beat.

Soul Food

Collard greens, black-eyed peas, okra, boiled cabbage, sweet potatoes, lima beans, red beans and rice, fried corn, chitlins, neck bones, ham hocks, pig tails, catfish, salmon croquettes, head cheese, fried chicken, tongue, grits, corn bread, hot sauce, hot peppers, boiled peanuts, gumbo, biscuits and redeye gravy, tea cakes, peach cobbler, corn fritters, banana pudding, rhubarb pie, fried pies, hush puppies. These foods, which are traditionally thought of as "southern," are part of Africa's and African Americans' contributions to world cuisine.

Traditional cooking, called soul food, is seasoned in part with fatback, which is salted or smoked pork fat from the back of the hog. The fatback is placed in the water with vegetables, such as greens, peas, beans, and cabbage to add flavor. Because of growing health consciousness, some African American cooks today are using smoked turkey instead of fatback to add flavor while reducing fat.

Spices play an important role in African American cooking, as they do in many hot-weather cultures. Mildly flavored food does not win high marks. As the saying goes, African Americans want to be able to "taste" their food. So food has to be highly seasoned to meet the approval of real soul food lovers. Bottles of hot sauce and hot peppers are usually included among the seasonings on the table to add an extra kick to the taste.

Certain meals and foods are considered traditional. The New Year's Day meal is one of them. Particular foods are eaten to ensure a good year. Greens are eaten to attract money; black-eyed peas and rice (called Hoppin' John) are eaten for good luck, as is pork. Corn bread is for health, and sweet potatoes are also usually part of the meal.

Sharing food is another tradition in African American culture. Taking a pot of food

---

HOPPIN' JOHN

6 cups water
1 pound dried black-eyed peas
8 ounces salt pork
1 large green pepper, chopped
1 large onion, chopped
6 cloves minced garlic

1 teaspoon ground cumin
1 teaspoon dried thyme
6 ounces tomato paste
1 teaspoon chili powder
2 cups uncooked rice
salt and pepper to taste

Cook the black-eyed peas in water in a large saucepan about one hour until tender. Add more water if necessary. Brown the salt pork over medium heat in a skillet. Add green pepper, onion, garlic, cumin, and thyme. Stir and cook until brown. Add tomato paste and chili powder and stir. Add a little water. Stir. Pour in the beans. Add rice and stir. Add enough water to cover mixture by about 1 1/2 inches. Cover and bring to a boil. Reduce heat and let simmer for thirty minutes. Add salt and pepper to taste. Serves six to eight people.

— Adapted from *The Black Family Reunion Cookbook* New York: Simon and Schuster, 1991.

to the home of a person who is sick or to help feed the family of someone who has died is a practice that still exists, although it is not as common now. If someone visits a home, it is customary to offer that individual something to eat. And if someone stops by during mealtime, you are expected to invite him or her to eat, even if you haven't "put their name in the pot," or cooked enough food to feed them.

Entertainment Based in West Africa

Sam Phillips, the founder of Sun Records — a label created to record blues musicians — once said he wished he could find a white singer with a Black sound for his label.

His wish came true when he discovered Elvis Presley — who later became known as the King of Rock 'n' Roll. The Black sound Sam Phillips was looking for is rooted in the rhythms, songs, and style of West African music. This music has more than one beat going at the same time and uses call and response, a style in which a lead person sings a line and the chorus replies by repeating the line, answering a question asked by the lead singer, or commenting on what the lead singer said. In addition, the singer may slide or slur from one note to the next, vocally leap from note to note, or use falsetto (a high-pitched style used by male singers). Improvisation, or unrehearsed additions to a song that add personal touches to the music, are also common in West African music.

In Africa, music is part of everyday life, part of people's work, play, and religious life. People sing when they're happy, when they're sad, or to pass the time of day. Its primary purposes are to record history, comment on

African American music has influenced music around the world. This music — rooted in the rhythms, song, and style of West African music — is the foundation of jazz, blues, rock 'n' roll, rap, gospel, and spirituals.

Games involving chanting, clapping, and dance movements are reminiscent of circle dances from West Africa.

events, record thoughts and feelings, and deepen the religious experience.

These songs are usually accompanied by dance. In fact, music and dance in Africa are like two sides of the same coin. People dance to express joy, sorrow, love, and anger, or to celebrate success or prevent bad luck. Each god has a dance, so dances are done for religious purposes as well as for fun.

Music Migrates

When African slaves were brought to this country, they carried this tradition of music and dance with them, a tradition that lives on in African American culture. The "field hollers" sung by slaves became spirituals, gospel, blues, ragtime, jazz, rhythm and blues, doo-wop, rap, and the a cappella (un-accompanied by instruments) singing style of groups such as Shai and Take Six.

Take Six. Singing a cappella (not accompanied by instruments) is a part of West African culture that continues in African American culture.

As in Africa, music is an important part of everyday life for most African Americans. The ability to sing and dance well is an admired talent in the African American community. Music in African American culture is not just something you listen to quietly; it's

West African dance styles, as performed by this African dance company, have influenced dances created by African Americans.

something you participate in. Audiences are expected to move to the groove (beat) of the music. Sometimes this might just involve bobbing the head or rocking side to side to the rhythm of the music. Other times, people may "dance" in their seats. And still other times, they may actually get up out of their seats and start dancing. If a certain part of the music appeals to someone, he or she may scream or shout out appreciation: "Go head," "Yes!," "Play it," "Sing it, baby." If the audience doesn't react to the music, the musicians feel they haven't touched the soul of their listeners.

Just as African American music is rooted in West Africa, so is dance. Many of the dances African Americans create have some of the same moves as African dance: They use glide, drag, or shuffle steps such as those used in the Electric Slide or Running Man. They may use jerking motions or involve pounding the feet on the ground, as in such dances as the Cool Jerk, Pop, Cabbage Patch or in tap dancing.

Other dances, such as the Twist or Butt, may involve pelvic movement, while still others, such as break dancing or the Snake, involve flexible, fluid body movements. A swinging rhythm in dances such as the Charleston, Butterfly, or Bart Simpson are also typical of African American dance. And always, there is room for improvisation.

BREAK DANCING: AN AFRICAN TRADITION?

A group of African Americans attending a national arts conference in Dakar, Senegal, went to a show featuring the country's national dance company. Among the dances performed was the Juggler's Dance. Two men who looked to be in their fifties did a dance that looked exactly like break dancing. When asked why break dancing had been included in an African dance performance, one of the hosts explained the Juggler's Dance was not break dancing, but a traditional Senegalese dance that was hundreds of years old.

Like African dance, most African American dances require minimal body contact. The exception to this is the slow dance (also known as the slow drag). Even in slow dancing, rhythm is important. The slow dance movement includes momentary pauses on the musical beat and gliding steps. In some instances, couples basically stand in one place and just move to the beat of the music.

Whether it's dance, music, food, language, or dress, understanding a racial or ethnic group's culture requires understanding its cultural roots. African Americans' cultural roots go back much further than American slavery. They go back to the mother continent, where creativity, originality, harmony with nature, and spiritual/religious values are the foundation upon which daily life is built.

Despite hundreds of years in this country, African Americans continue to live their lives in ways that reflect the values and traditions of Africa. This is what gives African Americans and African American culture style.

African-influenced dance may include jerking movements, gliding steps, or pounding the feet on the ground.

59

Chuck Berry is one of the pioneers of rock 'n' roll, which is rooted in African American music.

CHAPTER SIX

CONTRIBUTIONS TO AMERICAN CULTURE
"TO MAKE A POET BLACK AND BID HIM SING"

Anyone who questions whether African Americans have had an impact on American culture need only look at some of the ads McDonald's hamburger chain produced to appeal to the young people of the 1990s. The music, language, fashion, and style of these ads reflect hip-hop culture, which was created by African American youth living in the central city. The music of hip-hop is rap, which has a heavy emphasis on beat — an unmistakable link to West Africa.

But hip-hop music is not the only place to find the influences of African American culture on the broader culture. These influences show up in other forms of music, in art, theater, sports, science, politics — in short, in every facet of American life.

African American Music

The influence of African American culture in music is nothing new, nor is it limited to the U.S. British groups such as the Beatles and the Rolling Stones, and performers like Eric Clapton and Sting, have acknowledged the impact of African American music (ranging from blues and jazz to spirituals and gospel, and from rhythm and blues to rock 'n' roll) on their music. Jazz, which is commonly called America's classical music because it is considered by most experts to be the only music native to this country, is popular around the world — from Japan to Europe.

Jazz has had such an effect on U.S. culture that a period in history was named for it — the Jazz Age of the 1920s. It was during the Jazz Age that the Harlem Renaissance (also known as the Negro Renaissance) occurred. African American music, literature, and art flourished. European Americans from downtown traveled uptown to Harlem to hear African American jazz greats play in clubs that wouldn't admit African Americans.

AN UNUSUAL ALLIANCE

Wealthy European Americans — and some African Americans — held fancy parties to which the leading African American writers, musicians, and artists were invited to mingle with the "upper crust" in New York. Some of these wealthy individuals also helped support artists financially. The relationship between these supporters, known as patrons of the arts, and the artists was not always comfortable. In the case of Langston Hughes, for example, the poet did not like pressure from his patron, Charlotte Mason (whom he called "Godmother"), to write more about what she saw as the "primitive" (in her view, simple or uneducated) side of African American culture.

Duke Ellington, one of this country's foremost composers. His music ranges from popular to jazz to a blend of jazz and classical.

In 1939, opera singer Marian Anderson made history when she sang in front of seventy-five thousand people at the Lincoln Memorial.

From Slavery to the Classics. African American influence is not limited to jazz, rhythm and blues, gospel, spirituals, blues, and hip-hop. African Americans have also made their mark in classical music. Less than ten years after the end of slavery, African American singers were receiving recognition for their performance of European operatic music. The Hyer sisters, Anna Madah and Emma Louise, earned acclaim for their debut performance in Sacramento, California, in 1867. The sisters were only fourteen and sixteen years old. They toured throughout the United States and sang for royalty in Europe, winning high marks each time.

The first international operatic star was Sissieretta Joyner Jones. Jones, who made her debut in 1888, gave command performances for the Prince of Wales in England and President Benjamin Harrison at the White House.

In 1935, one of Europe's most famous conductors, Arturo Tuscanini, heard Marian Anderson sing in Salzburg, Austria. He was so impressed that he said "A voice such as this comes once in a hundred years." Despite her talent, Anderson still had to face open prejudice in her native land. In 1939, the Daughters of the American Revolution refused to let Anderson sing in Constitution Hall in Washington, D.C. First Lady Eleanor Roosevelt was so angered by this action that she resigned from the organization and arranged for Anderson to sing in an outdoor concert at the Lincoln Memorial. An estimated seventy-five thousand people, including members of the U.S. Supreme Court, Congress, and the cabinet, showed up for the concert.

On January 17, 1955, Marian Anderson became the first African American to sing at the Metropolitan Opera House. She paved the way for many other African American women opera singers, including Mattiwilda Dobbs, Grace Bumbry, Shirley Verrett, Clamma Dale, Kathleen Battle, Jessye Norman, and Leontyne Price, the first African American prima donna.

Women were not the only ones to earn a reputation for excellence as opera singers. Among the men were Roland Hayes, the son of slaves, who became the first African American to give a concert in Boston's Symphony Hall; George Shirley, who won the Metropolitan Opera audition in 1961; and William Warfield, a baritone whose concert performances were in demand throughout the world.

African American Themes. African Americans have also composed classical music and influenced European classical music. Much of the music composed by Louis Moreau Gottschalk (believed to be the first American composer of African ancestry to receive international recognition) is based on the Creole music and sounds of his native New Orleans. Scott Joplin, called the King of Ragtime music, also wrote the ragtime opera *Treemonisha*. While his shorter ragtime works were very popular, he could not convince music publishers and producers that an opera written by an African American around African American themes could be considered "serious" music.

Joplin died and was buried in an unmarked pauper's grave. But his music was rediscovered and regained popularity when his work was used in the 1973 Paul Newman and Robert Redford movie, *The Sting.*

From ragtime-influenced classical music to movies and Broadway musicals, the tradition of building music around African American themes and music has flourished. Edward Kennedy "Duke" Ellington was best known for songs like "Do Nothing 'Til You Hear From Me" and "Sophisticated Lady," both of which became jazz "standards" — works that are still performed today. Many of his works blended jazz with a classical music style.

The influence of African American music is also reflected in the film industry. In the thirties, forties, and fifties, the music most often heard in films was or sounded like European classical music. In some films, such as Walt Disney's *Fantasia,* animated charac-

AFRICAN AMERICAN LINGO: NO JIVE, JUST THE REAL McCOY

Many expressions in mainstream America have their origins in African American culture. The language of African Americans has contributed a large share of the many words and phrases that are taken for granted in American English. Here are some of them, with "translations" provided: Cool (together, okay), jive (deceptive, undependable), bad (good), laid back (not easily upset), sky (to jump high), right on (correct, yes), the man (person in position of power), deal (to cope with or handle), crib (home), gig (job), putdown (dismissal or rejection), ride (car), fox (attractive person), lame (ineffective or weak), slick (clever), dis (to disparage, dismiss, or insult), bump (to forget), cold (heartless), props (respect that has been earned), chill (to relax), large (wealthy), together (under control), and the real McCoy (genuine).

and other forms of African American music to theater audiences. Today, a great deal of the music written for film has its roots in African American music.

Quincy Jones helped introduce jazz and other African American music to film audiences through his innovative musical scores.

ters actually performed to famous classical works. In the 1960s, however, composers such as Quincy Jones started introducing jazz

African American Literature and Drama

In the 1920s, a brilliant social scientist named Dr. Charles Spurgeon Johnson helped set in motion a plan he believed would help tear down the wall of racism in this country. His unannounced plan was to replace racial stereotypes in literature with human truths told through the experiences of African American characters. He launched that plan on March 21, 1924, at the Civic Club in New York City, where a group of young African American writers had gathered to honor one of their own — Jessie Fauset.

At Last, a New Point of View. The works of these writers differed significantly from the traditional. Prior to this time, almost all literature written by African Americans reflected the images and style of European America. But these Harlem Renaissance writers produced works that reflected the images, style, and attitudes of *African* America. Writers such as poet Langston Hughes borrowed images from Africa and from African American family life. His work also reflects the strong influence of music on literature.

The list of Harlem Renaissance writers is long and illustrious. In addition to Hughes, it includes James Weldon Johnson, whose poetic sermons capture the style of the Black preacher — a style put to powerful use by Jesse Jackson and the late Rev. Dr. Martin Luther King, Jr. The list also includes Zora Neale Hurston, whose work reflecting the African

Poet Langston Hughes was one of the major writers to come out of the Harlem Renaissance of the 1920s.

American folk tradition has inspired contemporary African American writers, including Alice Walker and Noble Laureate Toni Morrison.

In the years following the Harlem Renaissance, such literary giants as Ralph Ellison, Richard Wright, and James Baldwin kept alive the use of African American experience as a basis for stories about the human experience. Today, not only general literature but even science fiction and children's literature have tapped into African American wit, wisdom, and lore as key ingredients in the stories they tell.

A Flair for the Dramatic. African American culture has also been reflected in drama, both on Broadway and off. The first African American to win the New York Drama Circle Critic's Award was Lorraine Hansberry, whose play *A Raisin in the Sun* was about the efforts

Nobel Prize-winning writer Toni Morrison bases her works on African American life and culture.

of a working-class African American family to better themselves.

African American culture is also overlaid on theater works that do not deal with African

Ralph Ellison's acclaimed *Invisible Man* captured the isolation African Americans feel in this country and won him the National Book Award for fiction in 1952.

Richard Wright, godfather to such literary giants as Ralph Ellison and James Baldwin, used his life experiences to write stories about the effects of racial injustice on the human spirit.

A Raisin in the Sun, by Lorraine Hansberry, was the first play by an African American to win the New York Drama Circle Critic's Award.

American lives. One major Broadway hit, *The Wiz,* retold *The Wizard of Oz* with a definite soulful flair. The stage version starred Stephanie Mills, and the film version starred Diana Ross and Michael Jackson.

Theater productions are not limited to Broadway. All over the country, African American theater companies are producing classic drama by African American playwrights, Black adaptations of non-African American works, and original pieces. In fact, much of the new drama by and about African Americans is being written and produced at these regional theaters.

Moving Back to Origins. Finally, modern African American literature is moving ever closer to its roots — the oral tradition of storytelling. The number of professional African American storytellers is growing rapidly. Their stories are based on traditional African and African American folktales, as well as more original, contemporary works.

These storytellers don't read their works but rather act them out for audiences in schools, libraries, and other locations around the country.

African American Art

Expression through the visual arts is not something new for people of African ancestry. Bronze and clay sculptures that portray complex religious themes are part of a Benin (West Africa) tradition that is thousands of years old. Benin bronze sculpture is regarded as among the most magnificent in the world and is in museums in Europe.

In Touch with the Homeland. Those who were transported to this country from Africa maintained many of the skills and the aesthetic eye of their homeland. Many items of art were functional and used for everyday living, such as grotesque jugs with facial features that were used to hold liquids; walking sticks carved with animals, humans, and other images similar to those found in West Africa; baskets woven in elaborate patterns; carved grave markers; and Voodoo objects.

Many slaves worked as silversmiths, furniture makers, blacksmiths, and tailors — making items that provided a more elegant lifestyle for the growing middle class in colonial America. Much of the elaborate decorative ironwork that decorates homes in New Orleans, Charleston, Savannah, Mobile, and other parts of the South were done by slaves.

The first well-known African American artists in this country lived in the nineteenth century. Among them were Joshua Johnston, who specialized in painting wealthy families in Baltimore; sculptor Edmonia Lewis; painter Robert Scott Duncanson, whose work included the famous painting of Uncle Tom and Little Eva; and Henry Ossawa Tanner, whose works include *The Banjo Lesson.*

Many early artists produced works in the style popular in Europe at the time. But others used themes that reflected their own heritage instead.

Acceptance of their work, regardless of which school of art they belonged to, was difficult because European Americans did not believe African Americans had the intellectual ability required to be true artists.

Pride and Protest. The strong move toward what was called Negritude — a reflection of racial pride, interest in African civilization, and a new understanding of what it means to be African American — began in the 1920s during the Harlem Renaissance. When the Great Depression came, European American patrons who had supported many of these artists no longer did so. When Franklin Roosevelt became president, however, he developed the Works Progress Administration (WPA), a program that put people back to work.

Among those included under this program were writers and artists. African American artists were hired to develop murals on public buildings. Out of this program came many of the giants of twentieth century African American art — painters Aaron Douglas, Charles White, Horace Pippen, and Jacob Lawrence; collage artist Romare Bearden; and sculptor Augusta Savage, to name a few.

During the 1950s and 1960s, a number of African American artists adopted a social protest theme in their work. Art became a way to raise and address issues that affected the lives of ordinary people. Today, "message" art is not as widespread, but using African and African American images and themes is still common.

Filmmaker Spike Lee helped pave the way for a new generation of African American filmmakers in the 1980s and 1990s.

African Americans are not restricted to art that is culturally based, however. They also produce abstract art, still lifes and other works that do not have a racial theme, and art by African Americans has grown in popularity among audiences and collectors of all ethnic groups.

Film

Filmmaker Spike Lee once called movies the most powerful medium in the world and said that African Americans could not afford to let other people control the images that define what it means to be African American.

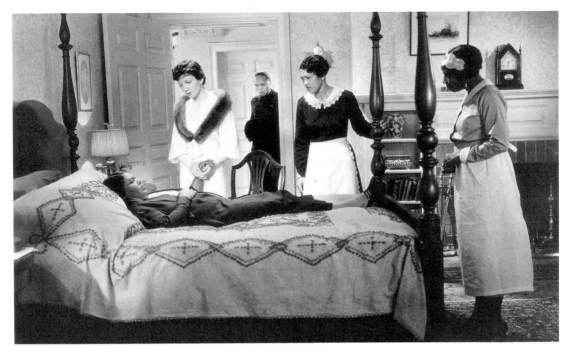

The Depression-era movie *Imitation of Life* deals with the subject of African Americans who pass for white to avoid the limitations and discrimination that life in America holds for people of color.

An Image Problem. Indeed, the image of African Americans projected on film has frequently been negative. During the silent film era, movies such as D. W. Griffith's *Birth of a Nation* portrayed African Americans as power-hungry, sex-crazed looters. Other early films stereotyped African Americans as stupid, irresponsible, lazy buffoons who slurred their speech and rolled their eyes, superstitious people who were afraid of their own shadow, or tragic victims. African Americans were usually cast in servant roles — as maids, butlers, or "mammies" who took care of children.

The images were so demeaning they prompted the creation of 150 independent film companies — many of them African American-owned — that produced everything from all-Black westerns and detective stories to romances, musicals, and melodramas. These "race" films, as they were called, were shown in segregated movie houses in the South, in movie houses in the urban North, and sometimes in churches and schools. The films were designed to show the positive side of the African American community. Among the films were *The Realization of a Negro's Ambition* and *Trooper K of Troop K,* both released in 1916.

The beginning of talking films prompted mainstream studios to make such movies as *Imitation of Life*, about a girl who passes for white to succeed in life, and *Green Pastures,* an idealized version of African American rural life. The images of African Americans set forth in these movies fought against the stereotype of African Americans as lazy fools whose principal function in life besides work was to entertain their masters.

A New Direction. One of the major figures in film during the 1930s was Paul Robeson, who also won acclaim as a singer.

Actor Sidney Poitier helped break new ground for African American film actors by playing intelligent, dignified, and honorable characters in dramatic roles.

The film that made Robeson an international star, *The Emperor Jones,* broke new ground by having Robeson in a starring role supported by a cast of white actors. Robeson played a proud, strong, cunning character who did not bow down to anyone — not even white men. The dramatic role was a major departure from the roles given to most African American males at that time. The film was so revolutionary it lost money and put its producers out of business.

Major changes in mainstream film did not happen until after World War II, when the NAACP and African American GIs — who had fought for freedom abroad that they did not have themselves at home — put pressure on the film industry to change the image of African Americans. The industry released several films — including *Home of the Brave* and *Intruders in the Dust* — that addressed the racial situation in the country.

In the 1950s, Sidney Poitier became the first major African American dramatic actor, playing dignified roles in films such as the *Defiant Ones,* which was about two escaped convicts — one black, one white — who are chained together and become "brothers" as a result of their experience during the escape attempt. In *Blackboard Jungle,* Poitier played an African American high school student who rebelled because he believed he would be treated like a second-class citizen by a society that did not give African Americans a chance to succeed.

Movies with an Attitude. In the 1960s, a more militant, action-oriented group of films began to emerge. These films came into their own in the early 1970s and included *Shaft* and *Superfly.* The heroes in these action movies were smart, tough men who beat the system. The movies usually took place in the ghetto and had a hard-edged, urban feel.

There were other films produced during this time, such as *Lady Sings the Blues* (the life story of singer Billie Holiday), *Sounder* (a story about the struggles of an African American family trying to survive during the Great Depression of the 1930s), *Buck and the Preacher* (a film about a former Union calvary officer leading a wagon train of former slaves to their new homes in the West), and *The Great White Hope* (the story of boxer Jack Johnson, the first African American heavyweight champion of the world).

But most of the films were what critics called "black exploitation" formula movies. They included *Superfly, Shaft's Big Score,* and

The first African American to become heavyweight champion of the world was Jack Johnson.

Coffy — movies that audiences grew tired of and stopped coming to see. When this happened, Hollywood stopped making films to appeal to African American audiences.

In the mid-1980s, the success of Spike Lee's *She's Gotta Have It* and Steven Spielberg's *The Color Purple* (based on the book by Alice Walker) renewed interest in films with African American themes and characters. In the 1990s, urban reality films, such as *Boyz 'n the Hood, New Jack City,* and *Menace II Society,* took up where the urban films of the 1970s had left off.

But that is not the end of the story. Other movies, such as Lee's *Malcolm X,* Julie Dash's *Daughters of the Dust,* and Charles Burnett's *To Sleep with Anger,* are moving film images in a different direction — to complex dramas that make no apologies for exploring the many and varied sides of African American life.

In an article appearing in *Ebony* magazine, Lee said it is important that African American filmmakers offer a variety of images that reflect the true diversity of the African American community.

African Americans in Sports

Sports are an important part of life in the African American community. The key position of sports in African American society can be traced back to Africa, where sports were part of every child's upbringing. Sports played many roles in African society, providing fitness and economic survival, as well as teaching military skills and cooperation with other members of the community. The principal sports were running, swimming, climbing, horseracing, boat racing, stick fighting, wrestling, gymnastics, and tug-of-war. Successful athletes were admired and given a place of respect —

particularly wrestlers, who were held in the same high regard as NBA basketball players today.

The Hard Road Up. In African American society, sports and sports figures also play several roles. One of the most important, especially in the early years, was as a symbol of the fight against an unjust system. When sports figures such as Jack Johnson, Joe Louis (who beat Max Schmeling — Adolf Hitler's "proof" of Aryan superiority), Muhammad Ali (who stood on principle against the Vietnam War and was stripped of his heavyweight title as a result), and Jackie Robinson (who broke the color barrier in major league baseball) beat the system, all African Americans felt they had beaten the system.

Sports in African American society is also seen as a way up and out of poverty. For a few people, that has been the case.

Given the number of African American professional athletes today, many people would believe success in sports has always come easily. But the reality is that the path to African Americans' achievement in professional sports has been, as the title of Arthur Ashe's three-volume history suggests, *A Hard Road to Glory*.

Not too many years ago, African American participation in major league baseball, basketball, football, and professional boxing was impossible. With the exception of boxing, African Americans were not able to compete in the other professional sports until this century. Modern major league baseball was not integrated until Jackie Robinson signed with the Brooklyn Dodgers in 1945. Basketball teams were not integrated until 1946, although there were a number of quality professional all-African American basketball teams that played against all-European Ameri-

Jackie Robinson, shown here greeting eager Dodger fans in Brooklyn, broke the color line in modern baseball when he became the first African American to play in the major leagues.

can teams. One of those teams is the Harlem Globetrotters, which still performs in the United States and abroad.

In 1902, Charles W. Follis became the first African American to play professional football, and in 1922 Fritz Pollard became the first African American NFL coach. But the NFL was barely integrated in the 1920s, and between 1934 and 1945, team owners used a variety of trumped-up excuses — including the supposed absence of African Americans talented enough to play pro ball — to bar African Americans from the NFL.

Lots of Ground to Cover. African Americans also experienced discrimination in track and field, mostly in the late nineteenth cen-

Jackie Joyner Kersee, considered the world's top female athlete, was the first to win the heptathlon in two consecutive Olympic games.

tury, when many amateur groups kept African American athletes out of competition.

Since that time, African Americans have made their mark in track and field. These athletes include Jesse Owens (who showed up Adolf Hitler by winning four gold medals in the 1936 Berlin Olympics), Wilma Rudolph (who became the first woman to win three gold medals in the 1960 Olympics), Carl Lewis (who, in 1984, became the first Olympian since Jesse Owens to win four gold medals in one Olympics), Jackie Joyner Kersee (a two-time Olympic winner in the heptathlon), and Edwin Moses (who won more than one hundred consecutive races in the four hundred-meter hurdles).

Baseball, basketball, football, boxing, track and field — these are all sports with which African Americans have become closely identified. And yet names like Althea Gibson

In 1960, Wilma Rudolph became the first American woman runner to win three gold medals in the Olympics. Twenty-seven years later she lit the torch during opening ceremonies at the Pan American Games in Indianapolis.

and Arthur Ashe (tennis) and Charles Sifford, Lee Elder, and Calvin Peete (golf) testify to two facts. One is that African Americans have made inroads in sports that have traditionally excluded them; the other is that their numbers remain few, so a great deal of ground has yet to be gained. And yet, despite the few African Americans who have broken into the pro ranks of these and other sports, another fact has also become clear: On the rinks, roadways, slopes, schoolyards, waterways, and playing fields of every type — in ice hockey, skiing, soccer, bowling, cycling, fencing, and crew — African Americans are contributing to the sporting life of all Americans. And in this way, they are also carrying on the traditional love of athletic competition rooted in the homeland — Africa.

Arthur Ashe became the first African American male to win the singles title at Wimbledon.

The first African American to play in the prestigious Wimbledon Tennis tournament was Althea Gibson.

Science and Technology

When it comes to science and technology, few people think about African Americans. Yet, as is the case with every other aspect of life in this country, African Americans have played a role.

Lighting the Way. African Americans invented a lot of the things we use and take for granted today. The first traffic light and gas mask were invented by Garrett A. Morgan. Lewis H. Latimer invented the carbon filament used by Thomas A. Edison to develop his incandescent light bulb.

Frederick M. Jones created the first refrigeration unit for trucks and the first portable x-ray machine. Granville T. Woods invented a

ONE LITTLE INVENTION, A BIG HIT FOR GOLF

Golf is a sport that has not been traditionally associated with African Americans. One little known fact is that the patent for the first golf tee (the little thing that holds the ball in place so the golfer can hit it) went to Dr. George F. Grant, a prominent African American dentist who received his degree from Harvard University. Dr. Grant invented the tee in 1899. Before this invention, golfers had to build up a little mound of dirt to elevate the ball each time they took their first shot at a hole.

Although this African American invention helped improve the game, African Americans were not welcome, and in some places are *still* not welcome, on golf courses owned by European Americans — except, of course, as caddies handing white golfers their clubs.

system that helped train engineers figure out how close they were to other trains and transmit messages between moving trains. He also invented the first egg incubator and a method for operators to talk or use Morse code on telegraph networks. Many of his inventions were sold to the Bell System, Westinghouse, and General Electric.

From Sugar to Shoe Soles. People who like sugar can thank Norbert Rillieux for inventing the machine that refines sugar. And everyone who wears shoes can thank Jan Ernst Matzeliger for inventing the machine that connects the soles of shoes to the uppers.

An African American, Dr. Daniel Hale Williams, was the first to do open heart surgery. Another, Dr. Charles Drew, discovered how to store blood in the form of plasma until it was needed. Ironically, Dr. Drew bled to death after a car accident when he was denied admission to a white hospital.

The first brain surgery on an unborn baby twin was done by Dr. Benjamin S. Carson, Sr., who, at forty-three, is considered one of this country's leading children's brain surgeons. William Cannady owns a business that helps match organ donors and recipients; the business is the third or fourth largest in the world.

Showing the Lay of the Land. An African American, Benjamin Banneker, surveyed the land and helped lay out the streets and buildings in Washington, D.C. And as a member of the first expedition to establish a camp base at the North Pole, Matthew Henson is believed to have reached the pole forty-five minutes before leader Robert E. Peary.

African Americans hold thousands of patents for inventions and processes that have helped make life easier, healthier, and safer all over the world. Yet, very little information about these individuals is known.

The contributions of African Americans in science, engineering, medicine, and research are all the more remarkable, given the fact that most have not been encouraged to pursue education and training in these areas. But African American organizations such as the National Technical Association are trying to change this by getting more young African American men and women interested in scientific, engineering, and technical fields as careers.

While success has not come easily for African Americans in science, technology, the arts, entertainment, or sports, it has come because of the determination and commitment of those who pioneered and those who followed.

CHRONOLOGY

1526 The first Africans are brought to South Carolina by a Spanish explorer to build a settlement. They escape to the interior of the state and live with American Indians.

1619 Twenty African indentured servants arrive in Jamestown, Virginia — the first to be brought to the English colonies.

1641 Massachusetts becomes the first colony to legalize slavery.

1767 With the printing of her poem "The University of Cambridge in New England," Phillis Wheatley, a fourteen-year-old slave, becomes the first African American to have her work published in America.

1770 Crispus Attucks, a runaway slave, becomes the first person to die in the American Revolution. He is shot by British soldiers during the Boston Massacre.

1787 Richard Allen, a former slave, founds the African Methodist Episcopal Church (the first denomination established by people of African descent in this country) in a blacksmith shop.

1804 Ohio passes the first "Black Laws" that restrict the rights and movement of African Americans.

1820 Eighty-six African Americans sail to West Africa to colonize Liberia, a nation founded through the efforts of the American Colonization Society and settled mainly by freed American slaves.

1821 The African Company theater troupe performs Shakespeare in New York.

1822 The slave revolt planned by Denmark Vesey in Charleston, South Carolina, is prevented when a slave reveals the plan. Vesey and thirty-six others are hanged.

1827 The first African American newspaper — *Freedoms Journal* — is published.

1863 President Abraham Lincoln issues the Emancipation Proclamation, which declares the freedom of all slaves held in states that have joined the Confederacy against the Union in the Civil War.

1870 Joseph Rainey of South Carolina becomes the first African American to serve in the House of Representatives. Hiram Rhoades Revels of Mississippi becomes the first African American to serve in the Senate.

1881 The "Jim Crow" railroad seating law is passed by Tennessee, thereby legalizing the segregation of African Americans within various walks of life. Booker T. Washington founds the Tuskegee Institute — a school established to train African American teachers. Lewis Latimer obtains a patent for the first incandescent electric light using a carbon filament.

1887 The Union Giants, the first African American baseball team, are organized in Chicago.

1891 Dr. Daniel H. Williams starts Provident Hospital in Chicago — first to train African American nurses.

1909 The National Association for the Advancement of Colored People (NAACP) is founded in New York.

1910 Jack Johnson becomes the first African American heavyweight champion of the world.

1917 About ten thousand African Americans walk down Fifth Avenue in New York in silent protest against lynching and riots in East St. Louis, Illinois.

1920s The Harlem Renaissance begins in New York.

1924 The Immigration Act is passed, preventing Africans from entering the United States.

1925 Malcolm X (born Malcolm Little) is born.

1926 Negro History Week is established by Dr. Carter G. Woodson.

1927 The legendary Harlem Globetrotters basketball team begins play.

1928 Oscar Depriest of Illinois is the first African American to be elected to congress from a northern state.

1929	Dr. Martin Luther King, Jr., is born.
1930	The Nation of Islam is founded by W. D. Fard.
1941	Dorie Miller, a messman on the *USS Arizona*, shoots down four Japanese planes with a machine gun during the attack on Pearl Harbor. He receives the Navy Cross for his heroism.
1950	Poet Gwendolyn Brooks becomes the first African American to win the Pulitzer Prize.
1954	The Supreme Court rules 9-0 to declare "separate but equal" schools unconstitutional.
1955	Montgomery bus boycott begins after Rosa Parks is arrested for refusing to give her seat to a white man.
1956	Tennis player Althea Gibson becomes the first African American to win a Grand Slam event when she triumphs in the women's singles and doubles at the French Open.
1963	Medgar Evers, head of the Mississippi NAACP, is murdered in the doorway of his home. The March on Washington to end discrimination is held. Dr. Martin Luther King, Jr., delivers his famous "I Have a Dream" speech during the largest protest in the nation's history.
1964	Dr. Martin Luther King, Jr., receives the Noble Peace Prize.
1965	Malcolm X is assassinated.
1966	Constance Baker Motley becomes the first African American female to be appointed a federal judge. Emmett Ashford becomes the first African American umpire to work a major league baseball game. The Black Panther Party is established in Oakland, California, by Huey Newton and Bobby Seale.
1967	Thurgood Marshall becomes the first African American to serve on the U.S. Supreme Court. Carl Stokes becomes the first African American to be elected mayor of a major American city — Cleveland.
1968	Dr. Martin Luther King, Jr., is assassinated.
1969	Charles Evers, brother of slain civil rights leader Medgar Evers, is elected mayor of Fayette, Mississippi.
1974	Hank Aaron becomes all-time home run leader when he hits number 715, breaking Babe Ruth's record.
1975	The first African American-owned and -operated television station — WGPR-TV in Detroit — goes on the air. Arthur Ashe becomes the first African American male to win the singles title at Wimbledon.
1992	Carol Moseley Braun is the first African American women elected to the United States Senate.

GLOSSARY

Afro	Also known as the "natural"; a hair style worn by some African Americans, most of whom have curly hair. The hair, which is kept curly, may vary in length but generally has a rounded shape.
Ashe	An inner spirituality, peace, strength, sophistication, nobility, and control.
Call and response	A worship style in which a congregation responds to preaching or singing by repeating what is said or by making verbal comments of approval.
The dozens	A verbal contest in which the goal is to make the most clever and cutting remark about the opponent or members of his/her family, other than the mother.
Driver	Black foreman on a plantation whose job was to make sure the slaves did their work and to keep the master informed about what was happening among the slaves and the white overseer.
Falsetto	A high-pitched style of singing by men.

Free papers   The papers African American slaves had to carry at all times to prove they were not slaves.

Free people of color   African American men, women, and children freed after serving time as indentured servants, being freed from slavery by their masters, or being born to free people.

Griot   The oral historian and keeper of traditions in West African culture.

Harlem Renaissance   A period during the 1920s in Harlem, New York, when African American art, music, and literature flourished.

Hip hop culture   A popular youth culture created by urban African Americans that includes a particular style of dress (loose-fitting and colorful), music (rap), and language.

Indenture   A contract for service between two people for a specific time period.

Jazz   A style of music created by African Americans that includes multiple rhythms, complex harmony, and improvisation.

Jumping the broom   A rite used by slaves to symbolize their marriage to each other. The man and woman jumped over a broom held a few inches off the ground while holding each other's hands.

Mammy   The house slave who was responsible for taking care of the master's children.

Middle Passage   The long voyage that brought most Africans to the Americas. The slaves were tightly packed below deck for most of the voyage. Millions died — so many that sharks followed the ships to eat the bodies of dead slaves thrown overboard on the trip from Africa.

Peacock revolution   The influence of African American men's styles of colorful dress and jewelry on European American men.

Plantation   A large farm on which workers live and raise crops.

Segregation   The separation of people based on their race or other factors.

Shout   An emotional response to a religious service brought on when one is overcome by the Holy Ghost (Holy Spirit).

Soul food   Traditional, well-seasoned African American food.

Woofing   A false threat or challenge issued as a high-powered joke, usually during a contest.

FURTHER READING

Ashe, Arthur. *A Hard Road to Glory: A History of the African-American Athlete.* Vol 1, *1619-1918.* Vol. 2, *1919-1945.* Vol. 3, *1946-Present.* New York: Warner Books, Inc., 1988.

Bennett, Lerone, Jr. *The Shaping of Black America.* Chicago: The Johnson Publishing Company, 1975.

Hughes, Langston. *Don't You Turn Back.* New York: Alfred Knopf, 1969.

Jacobs, Harriet A. *Incidents in the Life of a Slave Girl.* Cambridge: Harvard University Press, 1987.

Jones, Howard. *Mutiny on the Amistad.* Oxford: Oxford University Press, 1987.

Parks, Rosa. *Rosa Parks: My Story.* New York: Dial Books, 1992.

Taulbert, Clifton. *The Last Train North.* Tulsa: Council Oak Books, 1992.

Taulbert, Clifton. *Once Upon A Time When We Were Colored.* Tulsa: Council Oak Books, 1989.

Turner, Glennette. *Running for Our Lives.* New York: Holiday House, 1994.

Williams, Michael W., ed. *The African American Encyclopedia.* 6 vols. New York: Marshall Cavendish Corporation, 1993.

Woods, Paula, and Felix Liddell. *I, Too, Sing America.* New York: Workman Publishing, 1992.

INDEX

Bur.
19.95

PORTLAND PUBLIC LIBRARY

3 1220 00532 1473

W

j305.896 P347
Payton, Shelia.
African Americans

BURBANK BRANCH LIBRARY
377 STEVENS AVE.
PORTLAND, ME 04103

	DATE DUE	
NOV 1 0 1995	OCT 0 6 2001	
DEC 1 2 1995	NOV 0 1 2001	
	JUN 2 2 2004	
FEB 0 0 1996	JAN 2 5 2007	
MAR 2 1 1996	APR 1 2 2007	
RIU		
NOV 2 5 1998		
FEB 2 5 1999		